The
"I LOVE MY INSTANT POT®" Gluten-Free
Recipe Book

From *Zucchini Nut Bread* to *Fish Taco Lettuce Wraps*, 175 Easy and Delicious Gluten-Free Recipes

Michelle Fagone of CavegirlCuisine.com

Author of *The "I Love My Instant Pot®" Paleo Recipe Book*

Adams Media

New York   London   Toronto   Sydney   New Delhi

To Sam.
Thank you for fiercely loving me even when I'm mean. XOXO

Adams Media
An Imprint of Simon & Schuster, Inc.
57 Littlefield Street
Avon, Massachusetts 02322

First Adams Media trade paperback edition October 2018

ADAMS MEDIA and colophon are trademarks of Simon & Schuster.

For information about special discounts for bulk purchases, please contact Simon & Schuster Special Sales at 1-866-506-1949 or business@simonandschuster.com.

The Simon & Schuster Speakers Bureau can bring authors to your live event. For more information or to book an event contact the Simon & Schuster Speakers Bureau at 1-866-248-3049 or visit our website at www.simonspeakers.com.

Interior design by Michelle Kelly
Photographs by James Stefiuk

Manufactured in the United States of America

10 9 8 7 6 5 4 3 2 1

Library of Congress Cataloging-in-Publication Data
Fagone, Michelle, author.
The "I love my Instant Pot®" gluten-free recipe book / Michelle Fagone of CavegirlCuisine.com, author of The "I love my Instant Pot®" paleo recipe book.
Avon, Massachusetts: Adams Media, 2018.
Series: "I love my".
Includes index.
LCCN 2018022503 | ISBN 9781507208717 (pb) | ISBN 9781507208724 (ebook)
Subjects: LCSH: Gluten-free diet--Recipes. | Pressure cooking. | Electric cooking. | Celiac disease. | LCGFT: Cookbooks.
Classification: LCC RM237.86 .F34 2018 | DDC 641.5/639311--dc23
LC record available at https://lccn.loc.gov/2018022503

ISBN 978-1-5072-0871-7
ISBN 978-1-5072-0872-4 (ebook)

Contains material adapted from the following titles published by Adams Media, an Imprint of Simon & Schuster, Inc.: The "I Love My Instant Pot®" Recipe Book by Michelle Fagone, copyright © 2017, ISBN 978-1-5072-0228-9 and The "I Love My Instant Pot®" Paleo Recipe Book by Michelle Fagone, copyright © 2017, ISBN 978-1-5072-0574-7.

Contents

Introduction

The word *gluten* seems to be everywhere today. But it isn't just a fad word. In addition to celiac disease, there are many reasons to eat gluten-free. For example, ridding your body of gluten assists in stomach issues such as gas, bloating, and leaky gut syndrome. Since you will be eliminating many processed foods, you'll also find that weight loss can be a perk of this lifestyle. As you trade out processed foods for clean and fresh alternatives, your body will thank you with higher energy and better sleep. The pain of arthritis and other ailments due to inflammation can also be alleviated.

So, what is gluten exactly? Simply put, it is the protein found in wheat, rye, spelt, and barley that is used in products like bread, pasta, and tortillas. But it is not just these bready products that should be avoided. Gluten is also hidden in condiments such as soy sauce, ketchup, and mustard. A lot of these condiments, as well as sauces, processed meats, and even coffee substitutes, use flour gluten as a filler or stabilizer for a longer shelf life. So, by giving up gluten, you'll be giving up a large amount of processed foods as well, thereby ridding your body of the many toxins found in the food on grocery store shelves. Give it just two weeks and you'll start to fully feel the health benefits!

And that's where your Instant Pot® comes in. Cooking with an Instant Pot® is a life-changing experience, especially when you follow a gluten-free lifestyle, because when you cook your own meals, you know absolutely what the recipe ingredients are! This multifunction cooking tool allows you to sauté, brown, steam, and warm your food. It cooks soups, eggs, and even cakes! And the high-pressure cooking and steaming ability of an Instant Pot® does wonders to steak, pork shoulder, and chicken. With the touch of a button you'll be able to cook cuts of meat that would normally take hours in just minutes. The Instant Pot® cooks food at a low temperature, but it does it more efficiently than other slow-cooking methods or appliances because it also uses pressure and steam. It is like a pressure cooker and a slow cooker rolled into one. This cooking method also seals in essential vitamins and minerals and allows the Instant Pot® to turn out healthier, better-tasting food that is perfect when you're on the go.

Whether you've just bought your Instant Pot® or have been using one for years and just need some inspiration, this book is for you. Inside you'll find 175 delicious gluten-free recipes ranging from Southern Breakfast Grits and Three-Bean Chili to Mini Reuben Potato Skins and Hearty Garlic Mushrooms. You'll also find decadent desserts, including Strawberry Cupcakes with Vanilla Buttercream and Lime Cheesecake. The more you cook, the more you'll realize how versatile the Instant Pot® really is, whether you're making a hearty breakfast, an amazing main course, or a delicious dessert. So, plug in your Instant Pot® and get ready to enjoy some amazing, delicious, and quick gluten-free meals.

Cooking with an Instant Pot®

So you're about to venture into the amazing world of Instant Pot® cooking...but you're not sure where or how to start. Don't worry; this chapter will give you the information you need to get started. Here you'll learn what all those buttons on your Instant Pot® do, how to release the pressure from the Instant Pot® when the cooking time is up, how to keep your Instant Pot® clean, and more.

Even though you'll learn all this information in this chapter, it's important that you read the owner's manual as well. That user manual is your key to successfully creating the recipes throughout this book. In addition to pointing out the basic functions of the appliance, it will tell you how to do an initial test run using water to get familiar with the Instant Pot®. I can't stress enough that you need to do this. It will both familiarize you with the appliance and take away some of your anxiety. In addition, this first run will help steam clean your pot before you use it to make your favorite recipe.

But for now, let's take a look at some Instant Pot® basics.

Function Buttons

You are staring at the Instant Pot®, and there are so many buttons. Which one should you use? Most of the function buttons seem obvious, but it is important to note that several are set with preprogrammed default cooking times. Also, keep in mind that every button option on the Instant Pot® is programmed with a 10-second delay, meaning that cooking begins 10 seconds after you hit the button. Most likely you will use the Manual or Pressure Cook button the most because you will have more control, but read on for more detailed information regarding the remaining function buttons.

Manual/Pressure Cook button. Depending on the model of Instant Pot®, there is a button labeled either Manual or Pressure Cook. This might be the most-used button on the Instant Pot®. The default pressure setting is High; however, you can toggle the pressure from High to Low by pressing the Pressure button. Use the Plus and Minus buttons to adjust the pressurized cooking time.

Sauté button. This button helps the Instant Pot® act as a skillet for sautéing vegetables or searing meat prior to adding the remaining ingredients of a recipe, and it is used for simmering sauces as well. There are three temperature settings—Normal, Less, and More—that can be accessed using the Adjust button. The Normal setting is for sautéing, the Less setting is for simmering, and the More setting is for searing meat.

Keep the lid open when using the Sauté button to avoid pressure building up.

Soup button. This button is used to cook soups and broths at high pressure for a default of 30 minutes. The Adjust button allows you to change the cooking time to 20 or 40 minutes.

Porridge button. This button is used to cook porridge, congee, and *jook* in the Instant Pot® at high pressure for a default of 20 minutes. The Adjust button allows you to change the cooking time to 15 or 40 minutes.

Poultry button. This button is used to cook chicken, turkey, and even duck at high pressure for a default of 15 minutes. The Adjust button allows you to change the cooking time to 5 or 30 minutes.

Meat/Stew button. This button is used to cook red meats and stew meats at high pressure for a default of 35 minutes. The Adjust button allows you to change the cooking time to 20 or 45 minutes.

Bean/Chili button. This button is used to cook dried beans and chili at high pressure for a default of 30 minutes. The Adjust button allows you to change the cooking time to 25 or 40 minutes.

Rice button. This button is used to cook white rice such as jasmine or basmati at low pressure. The Instant Pot® will automatically set the default cooking time by sensing the amount of water and rice in the cooking vessel.

Multigrain button. This button is used to cook grains such as wild rice, quinoa, and barley at high pressure for a default of 40 minutes. The Adjust button allows you to change the cooking time to 20 or 60 minutes.

Steam button. This button is excellent for steaming vegetables and seafood using your steamer basket. It steams for a default of 10 minutes. The Adjust button allows you to change the cooking time to 3 or 15 minutes. Quick-release the steam immediately after the timer beeps so as to not overcook the food.

Slow Cook button. This button allows the Instant Pot® to cook like a slow cooker. It defaults to a 4-hour cook time. The Adjust button allows you to change the temperature to Less, Normal, or More, which correspond to a slow cooker's Low, Normal, or High. The Plus and Minus buttons allow you to adjust the cooking time.

Keep Warm/Cancel button. When the Instant Pot® is being programmed or in operation, pressing this button cancels the operation and returns the Instant Pot® to a standby state. When the Instant Pot® is in the standby state, pressing this button again activates the Keep Warm function.

Automatic Keep Warm function. After the ingredients in the Instant Pot® are finished cooking, the pot automatically switches over to the Keep Warm function and will keep your food warm up to 10 hours. This is perfect for large cuts of meat as well as for soups, stews, and chili, allowing the spices and flavors to really marry for an even better taste. The first digit on the LED display will show an L to indicate that the Instant Pot® is in the Keep Warm cycle, and the clock will count up from 0 seconds to 10 hours.

Timer button. This button allows you to delay the start of cooking up to 24 hours. After you select a cooking program and make any time adjustments, press the Timer button and use the Plus or Minus keys to enter the delayed hours; press the Timer button again and use the Plus or Minus keys to enter the delayed minutes. You can press the Keep Warm/Cancel button to cancel the timed delay. The Timer function doesn't work with Sauté, Yogurt, and Keep Warm functions.

How Does Food Cook in 0 Minutes?

If you are confused about how some recipes require 0 minutes to cook, it's not a typo. Some veggies and seafoods that require only minimal steaming are set at zero cooking time. Food can actually be cooked in the time that it takes the Instant Pot® to achieve pressure.

Locking and Pressure-Release Methods

Other than the Sauté function, where the lid should be off, and the Slow Cook or Keep Warm functions, where the lid can be on or off, most of the cooking you'll do in the Instant Pot® will be under pressure, which means you need to know how to lock the lid before pressurized cooking and how to safely release the pressure after cooking. Once your ingredients are in the inner pot

of the Instant Pot®, lock the lid by putting it on the Instant Pot® with the triangle mark aligned with the Unlocked mark on the rim of the Instant Pot®. Then turn the lid 30 degrees clockwise until the triangle mark on the lid is aligned with the Locked mark on the rim. Turn the pointed end of the pressure release handle on top of the lid to the Sealing position. After your cooking program has ended or you've pressed the Keep Warm/Cancel button to end the cooking, there are two ways you can release the pressure:

Natural-release method. To naturally release the pressure, simply wait until the Instant Pot® has cooled sufficiently for all the pressure to be released and the float valve drops, normally about 10–15 minutes. You can either unplug the Instant Pot® while the pressure releases naturally or let the pressure release while it is still on the Keep Warm function.

Quick-release method. The quick-release method stifles the cooking process and helps unlock the lid for immediate serving. To quickly release the pressure on the Instant Pot®, make sure you are wearing oven mitts, then turn the pressure release handle to the Venting position to let out steam until the float valve drops. This is generally not recommended for starchy items or large volumes of liquid (e.g., soup) so as to avoid any splattering that may occur. Be prepared, because the noise and geyser effect of the releasing steam during the quick-release method can be off-putting. Also, if you own dogs, this release is apparently the most frightening part of their day, so take caution.

Pot-in-Pot Accessories

Pot-in-pot cooking is when you place another cooking dish inside the Instant Pot® for a particular recipe. The Instant Pot® is straightforward and comes with an inner pot and steam rack; however, there are many other tricks and recipes that can be made with the purchase of a few other accessories, including a springform pan, cake pan, glass bowl, and ramekins.

7" springform pan. A 7" springform pan is the perfect size for making a cheesecake and many other desserts in an Instant Pot®. It is the right dimension to fit inside the pot, and it makes a dessert for four to six people.

6" cake pan. A 6" pan is excellent for making a small cake in the Instant Pot®. It can serve four to six people depending on the serving size. This pan is perfect for a family craving a small dessert without committing to leftovers.

7-cup glass bowl. A 7-cup bowl fits perfectly in the Instant Pot® and works great for eggs and bread puddings that generally would burn on the bottom of the pot insert. The items in the bowl sit up on the inserted steam rack and are cooked with the steam and pressure of the pot.

Ramekins. These baking dishes usually come in 4-ounce sizes and are the perfect vessels for tasty individual custards.

Steamer basket. A steamer basket helps create a raised shelf for steaming. Shop around, as there are several variations, including metal or silicone steamer baskets.

Some even have handles to make it easier to remove them after the cooking process.

Silicone baking cupcake liners. Silicone baking cupcake liners are great for mini meatloaves, cupcakes, on-the-go frittatas, and little quick breads.

Although these accessories can help you branch out and make different recipes with the Instant Pot®, there are many recipes you can make using just the inner pot and steam rack that come with your appliance. These are just handy items you can purchase along the way to use with what will soon become your favorite heat source in the kitchen.

Accessory Removal

Cooking pot-in-pot is a great idea until it's time to remove the inserted cooking dish. Because of the tight space, it is almost impossible to use thick oven mitts to reach down and grip something evenly without tipping one side of the cooking vessel and spilling the cooked item. There are a few ways around this:

Retriever tongs. Retriever tongs are a helpful tool for removing hot bowls and pans from the Instant Pot®.

Mini mitts. Small oven mitts are helpful when lifting pots out of an Instant Pot® after the cooking process, especially the type made of silicone. They are more heat-resistant and less cumbersome than traditional oven mitts, which can prove to be bulky in the tight space of the cooker.

Aluminum foil sling. This is a quick, inexpensive fix to the problem of lifting a heated dish out of an Instant Pot®. Take a 10" × 10" square of aluminum foil and fold it back and forth until you have a 2" × 10" sling. Place this sling underneath the bowl or pan before cooking so that you can easily lift up the heated dish.

Although necessary if you do pot-in-pot cooking, these retrieval tools are not needed if you are simply using the interior pot that comes with the appliance upon purchase. A slotted spoon will do the trick for most other meals.

Cleaning Your Instant Pot®

When cleaning up after using your Instant Pot®, the first thing you should do is unplug it and let it cool down. Then you can break down the following parts to clean and inspect for any trapped food particles:

Inner pot. The inner pot, the cooking vessel, is dishwasher safe; however, the high heat causes rainbowing, or discoloration, on stainless steel. To avoid this, hand-wash the pot.

Outer heating unit. Wipe the interior and exterior with a damp cloth. Do not submerge in water, as it is an electrical appliance.

Steam rack. The steam rack is dishwasher safe or can be cleaned with soap and water.

Lid. The lid needs to be broken down into individual parts before washing. The sealing ring, the float valve, the pressure release handle, and the antiblock shield all need to be cleaned in different ways:

- **Sealing ring.** Once this ring is removed, check the integrity of the silicone. If it is torn or cracked, it will not seal properly and may hinder the cooking process, in which case it should not be used. The sealing ring needs to be removed and washed each time because the ring has a tendency to hold odors when cooking. Vinegar or lemon juice is excellent for reducing odors. You can purchase additional rings for a nominal price. Many Instant Pot® users buy more than one ring and use one for meats and a separate one for desserts and milder dishes.

- **Float valve.** The float valve is a safety feature that serves as a latch lock that prevents the lid from being opened during the cooking process. Make sure this valve can move easily and is not obstructed by any food particles.

- **Pressure-release handle.** This is the venting handle on top of the lid. It can be pulled out for cleaning. It should be loose, so don't worry. This allows it to move when necessary.

- **Antiblock shield.** The antiblock shield is the little silver "basket" underneath the lid. It is located directly below the vent. This shield can and should be removed and cleaned. It blocks any foods, especially starches, so they don't clog the vent.

So, now that you know about all the safety features, buttons, and parts of the Instant Pot® and know how to clean everything, it's time for the fun part. The cooking process is where the excitement begins.

Breakfast and Gluten-Free Breads

Breakfast is one of the easiest meals to eat from a drive-thru. We are tired and in a rush, and we just don't have the time to put together something healthy. Unfortunately, there aren't many gluten-free fast-food options, and just eating the insides out of a breakfast sandwich can get messy, expensive, and boring. Fortunately, the Instant Pot® can save the day with its shortened cooking time, freeing you from having to stand over the skillet. All you have to do is add your ingredients, press a button, and go get ready to tackle your day. Try prepping some of the fruits and vegetables the night before so you can eliminate this step in the morning as well.

From muffins to eggs, this chapter has got you covered with a myriad of delicious, gluten-free breakfast recipes, including Mushroom and Goat Cheese Frittata, Southern Breakfast Grits, and Strawberries 'n' Cream Oats. And once you get comfortable with some of the basics, you should feel free to get creative and make some of your own morning masterpieces. So get cooking, and let your family wake up with a new appreciation for their soon-to-be-favorite kitchen gadget!

Mushroom and Goat Cheese Frittata

Although this recipe has specific ingredients, a frittata is perfect for any leftover veggies or odd pieces of cheese you are left with at the end of the week. The Instant Pot® helps bring all of those tasty bits together into the perfect bite of quick and healthy gluten-free food.

- **Hands-On Time: 10 minutes**
- **Cook Time: 13 minutes**

Serves 4

6 large eggs
¼ cup chopped fresh basil leaves
½ cup crumbled goat cheese
½ teaspoon salt
¼ teaspoon ground black pepper
1 tablespoon olive oil
2 cups sliced baby bella mushrooms
1 small yellow onion, peeled and diced
1 cup water

1 In a medium bowl, whisk together eggs, basil, goat cheese, salt, and pepper. Set aside.

2 Press the Sauté button on the Instant Pot®. Heat oil 30 seconds and stir-fry mushrooms and onions 5 minutes until onions are translucent.

3 Transfer cooked mushroom mixture to a 7-cup glass bowl greased with either oil or cooking spray and set aside to cool 5 minutes. Pour whisked eggs over the cooked mixture and stir to combine.

4 Add water to the Instant Pot® and insert steam rack. Place glass bowl with egg mixture on steam rack. Lock lid.

5 Press the Manual or Pressure Cook button and adjust cook time to 8 minutes. When timer beeps, let pressure release naturally until float valve drops and then unlock lid.

6 Remove dish from pot and set aside 10 minutes to allow the eggs to set. Slice and serve warm.

Crustless Artichoke and Kalamata Olive Quiche

Bring a little Greece to your breakfast table with this crustless quiche. The tangy flavor of the feta is a tried-and-true sidekick of the fruity yet briny flavor of the Kalamata olive. Taste aside, six of these little drupes contain as much fiber as an orange, which is perfect if you are on a gluten-free diet trying to compensate for the fiber you had to give up with whole-wheat breads.

- **Hands-On Time: 10 minutes**
- **Cook Time: 8 minutes**

Serves 6

6 large eggs
¼ cup whole milk
2 teaspoons chopped fresh dill
½ teaspoon salt
¼ teaspoon ground black pepper
1 Roma tomato, seeded and diced
¼ cup diced jarred artichokes, drained
¼ cup sliced pitted Kalamata olives
¼ cup crumbled feta cheese
¼ cup peeled and diced red onion
2 cups water

1 In a medium bowl, whisk together eggs, milk, dill, salt, and pepper. Stir in tomato, artichokes, olives, feta cheese, and onion. Set aside.

2 Add egg mixture to a 7-cup glass dish greased with either oil or cooking spray.

3 Add water to the Instant Pot®. Insert steam rack. Place dish with egg mixture on steam rack. Lock lid.

4 Press the Manual or Pressure Cook button and adjust cook time to 8 minutes. When timer beeps, let pressure release naturally for 10 minutes. Quick-release any additional pressure until float valve drops and then unlock lid.

5 Remove dish from pot and let sit 10 minutes. Slice and serve warm.

Squash Casserole Frittata

Squash casserole is a delicacy down South, served as a side at important family gatherings. This frittata is the perfect vehicle to deliver the tasty combination of flavors on a daily basis straight from your Instant Pot®—and your family won't believe it's gluten-free!

- **Hands-On Time: 10 minutes**
- **Cook Time: 8 minutes**

Serves 4

6 large eggs

2 tablespoons whole milk

2 slices gluten-free bread, cubed

1 teaspoon salt

½ teaspoon ground black pepper

¼ cup shredded Cheddar cheese

3 cups shredded yellow squash (approximately 1 large)

¼ cup peeled and diced sweet onion

1 cup water

1 In a medium bowl, whisk together eggs and milk. Stir in bread to soak up some of the liquid. Add salt, pepper, cheese, squash, and onion.

2 Transfer egg mixture to a 7-cup glass bowl greased with either oil or cooking spray.

3 Add water to the Instant Pot® and insert steam rack. Place glass bowl with egg mixture on steam rack. Lock lid.

4 Press the Manual or Pressure Cook button and adjust cook time to 8 minutes. When timer beeps, let pressure release naturally until float valve drops and then unlock lid.

5 Remove dish from pot and set aside 10 minutes to allow the eggs to set. Slice and serve warm.

Ham and Swiss Egg Muffins

These savory little comfort muffins are great on the run. And the ham and Swiss combo is undeniable. The sharp flavor of the Dijon mustard is the bow that ties this classic combination together. Skip the drive-thru, calories, and gluten-filled breading, and prep this simple, tasty breakfast instead.

- **Hands-On Time: 10 minutes**
- **Cook Time: 8 minutes**

Serves 6

4 large eggs
½ cup small-diced cooked ham
½ cup grated Swiss cheese
2 teaspoons Dijon mustard
½ teaspoon salt
½ teaspoon ground black pepper
1 cup water

1 In a medium bowl, whisk together eggs, ham, cheese, Dijon mustard, salt, and pepper. Distribute egg mixture evenly among six silicone cupcake liners lightly greased with either oil or cooking spray.

2 Add water to the Instant Pot® and insert steam rack. Place steamer basket on steam rack. Carefully place muffin cups in steamer basket. Lock lid.

3 Press the Manual or Pressure Cook button and adjust cook time to 8 minutes. When timer beeps, quick-release pressure until float valve drops and then unlock lid.

4 Remove egg muffins and serve warm.

Sausage and Onion Cheesy Egg Muffins

These make-ahead cheesy egg muffins are filled with flavor! Eat these right away, save for the morning, or freeze them for later. Eggs are a superfood with a long list of nutrients. They are the perfect protein to help stave off hunger pangs and boost energy until lunch and will help you avoid those gluten-filled donuts in the break room!

- **Hands-On Time: 10 minutes**
- **Cook Time: 13 minutes**

Serves 6

1 tablespoon olive oil

½ small yellow onion, peeled and diced

¼ pound ground pork sausage

4 large eggs

¼ cup grated mozzarella cheese

⅛ teaspoon salt

½ teaspoon ground black pepper

1 cup water

VARIETIES OF PORK SAUSAGE

All varieties of pork sausage work in this recipe—it is just a matter of your personal taste. If you like spice, try ground chorizo, a spicy blend found mostly in Mexican cuisine. If you are looking for a Mediterranean flavor, you can use Italian pork sausage. And then there is breakfast pork sausage, which is the most common mild sausage used in breakfast dishes.

1 Press the Sauté button on the Instant Pot® and heat oil 30 seconds. Add onion and sausage. Stir-fry 5 minutes until onions and sausage start to brown. Transfer mixture to a small bowl to cool while egg mixture is being prepared.

2 In a medium bowl, whisk together eggs, cheese, salt, and pepper. Stir cooled onion mixture into egg mixture. Distribute egg mixture evenly among six silicone cupcake liners lightly greased with either oil or cooking spray.

3 Add water to the Instant Pot® and insert steam rack. Place steamer basket on steam rack. Carefully place cupcake liners in steamer basket. Lock lid.

4 Press the Manual or Pressure Cook button and adjust cook time to 8 minutes. When timer beeps, quick-release pressure until float valve drops and then unlock lid.

5 Remove egg muffins and serve warm.

Savory Bacon and Goat Cheese Buckwheat Muffins

If you want a sweet and savory adventure, spread these luscious muffins with a little fig jam to spin your taste buds out of control. The onion in this recipe lends a moistness and flavor to these wheat-free muffins; however, if it doesn't set well with your gut, you can just skip it.

- **Hands-On Time: 5 minutes**
- **Cook Time: 15 minutes**

Serves 6

4 slices bacon, diced
½ small yellow onion, peeled and diced
1 cup buckwheat flour
2 teaspoons gluten-free baking powder
½ teaspoon baking soda
½ teaspoon ground black pepper
3 tablespoons unsalted butter, melted
2 large eggs, whisked
½ cup crumbled goat cheese
1 cup water

WHY BUCKWHEAT FLOUR IS GLUTEN-FREE

Don't let the word *wheat* in *buckwheat* scare you. Buckwheat is actually a seed, not a grain, and it lends a slightly bitter and beautifully rustic flavor to breads, pancakes, and even noodles. Read your labels though, as some brands blend buckwheat with other not-so-gluten-free flours.

1 Press the Sauté button on the Instant Pot®. Add bacon and onion to pot. Stir-fry 5 minutes until onions start to brown and bacon is crisp. Transfer mixture to a small bowl lined with a paper towel to cool until ready to use.

2 In a medium bowl, combine flour, baking powder, baking soda, pepper, butter, and eggs. Fold in goat cheese and cooled bacon mixture. Distribute mixture evenly among six silicone cupcake liners lightly greased with either oil or cooking spray.

3 Add water to the Instant Pot® and insert steam rack. Place steamer basket on steam rack. Carefully place cupcake liners in steamer basket. Lock lid.

4 Press the Manual or Pressure Cook button and adjust cook time to 10 minutes. When timer beeps, quick-release pressure until float valve drops and then unlock lid.

5 Remove muffins and serve warm.

Southern Breakfast Grits

Grits traditionally require a lot of salt to bring out the flavor; however, with the addition of bacon in this recipe, you can use a light hand on the salt. Ground down from corn, grits are a naturally gluten-free product. After stirring in the cheese and bacon, give the grits a quick taste test before ladling into everyone's bowl, and add more salt if needed.

- **Hands-On Time: 5 minutes**
- **Cook Time: 15 minutes**

Serves 6

4 slices bacon, diced
5 cups water
1 cup coarse corn grits
2 tablespoons unsalted butter
½ teaspoon salt
½ cup shredded sharp Cheddar cheese

1 Press the Sauté button on the Instant Pot®. Add bacon to pot. Stir-fry 5 minutes until bacon is crisp. Transfer bacon to a small plate lined with a paper towel to cool while grits are being prepared.

2 Stir water, grits, butter, and salt together in the Instant Pot®. Lock lid.

3 Press the Manual or Pressure Cook button and adjust cook time to 10 minutes. When timer beeps, allow pressure to release naturally for 3 minutes. Quick-release any additional pressure until float valve drops and unlock lid.

4 Whisk grits in pot 5 minutes until they thicken. Stir in cheese and cooked bacon.

5 Ladle grits into six bowls and serve.

Sawmill Gravy

Whether you serve it with gluten-free biscuits, morning home fries, or mashed potatoes, this gluten-free sausage gravy is the ideal savory addition to your brunch table. And why do they call it "Sawmill Gravy"? Well, the added cornmeal adds a little bit of "sawdust" to give it some grit!

- **Hands-On Time: 5 minutes**
- **Cook Time: 17 minutes**

Serves 10

2 tablespoons unsalted butter

1 pound ground pork sausage

1 small sweet onion, peeled and diced

¼ cup chicken broth

¼ cup gluten-free all-purpose flour

1 tablespoon cornmeal

1½ cups whole milk

½ teaspoon salt

1 tablespoon ground black pepper

1 Press the Sauté button on the Instant Pot®. Add butter to pot and heat 1 minute until melted. Add sausage and onion. Stir-fry 5 minutes until onions are translucent. The pork will still be a little pink.

2 Add chicken broth to the Instant Pot®. Lock lid.

3 Press the Manual or Pressure Cook button and adjust cook time to 1 minute. When timer beeps, quick-release pressure until float valve drops and then unlock lid.

4 Whisk in flour, cornmeal, milk, salt, and pepper. Press the Keep Warm button and let the gravy sit 10 minutes to allow the sauce to thicken, stirring occasionally.

5 Remove gravy from heat and serve warm.

Peanut Butter and Jelly Oatmeal

Rich in antioxidants and soluble fiber, oatmeal is a powerhouse starter to your day, especially when you're watching your gluten intake. The fiber in the oatmeal, as well as the peanut butter, gives your body the boost it has been craving. But don't tell the kiddos that it is good for them; just stir in a little PB&J and watch their smiles widen. This recipe is proof that healthy does not equal yucky!

- **Hands-On Time: 5 minutes**
- **Cook Time: 7 minutes**

Serves 2

1 cup old-fashioned oats

1¼ cups water

⅛ teaspoon salt

2 teaspoons smooth peanut butter

2 tablespoons strawberry jelly

¼ cup whole milk

1 Add oats, water, and salt to the Instant Pot®. Lock lid.

2 Press the Porridge button and adjust cook time to 7 minutes. When timer beeps, let pressure release naturally for 5 minutes. Manually release any additional pressure and unlock lid.

3 Transfer oatmeal to two bowls. Stir in peanut butter and jelly. Add milk. Serve warm.

Apple and Pecan Oatmeal

Apple-picking is a great outing for a family, but you are usually left trying to figure out what to do with an entire bag of apples. Besides eating them right out of the bag or making applesauce, you can dice some up and add them to a bowl of oatmeal. Along with the oatmeal, apples are a great form of fiber as well as phytonutrients and antioxidants. There's a reason why it is said they keep the doctor away!

- **Hands-On Time: 5 minutes**
- **Cook Time: 7 minutes**

Serves 2

1 cup old-fashioned oats

1¼ cups water

1 peeled and cored Granny Smith apple, diced

¼ teaspoon ground cinnamon

⅛ teaspoon salt

2 tablespoons light brown sugar

¼ teaspoon vanilla extract

¼ cup chopped pecans

4 tablespoons whole milk

1 Add oats, water, apple, cinnamon, and salt to the Instant Pot®. Lock lid.

2 Press the Porridge button and adjust cook time to 7 minutes. When timer beeps, let pressure release naturally for 5 minutes. Manually release any additional pressure and unlock lid. Stir in brown sugar and vanilla.

3 Transfer oatmeal to two bowls. Garnish with pecans. Pour milk over oatmeal. Serve warm.

Strawberries 'n' Cream Oats

Naturally gluten-free, strawberries add a nutritional boost of vitamin C and potassium! This creamy bowl of oats will warm not only your tummy but your heart as well. Get creative with this recipe by trying peaches, blueberries, or even bananas!

- **Hands-On Time: 5 minutes**
- **Cook Time: 7 minutes**

Serves 2

1 cup old-fashioned oats

1 cup water

½ cup whole milk

2 cups diced fresh strawberries, hulled

2 tablespoons granulated sugar

¼ teaspoon vanilla extract

¼ teaspoon ground cinnamon

⅛ teaspoon salt

1 Add oats, water, milk, strawberries, sugar, vanilla, cinnamon, and salt to the Instant Pot®. Stir to combine. Lock lid.

2 Press the Manual or Pressure Cook button and adjust cook time to 7 minutes. When timer beeps, quick-release pressure until float valve drops and then unlock lid.

3 Stir oatmeal and ladle into two bowls. Serve warm.

Nutty Chocolate Banana Quinoa Bowl

If you are bored of oatmeal, try a protein-packed quinoa bowl. This breakfast not only ups your protein; it also quenches your sweet tooth. You know that quinoa is full of fiber and is naturally gluten-free, but did you know that it is one of the rare foods that contains all nine essential amino acids, making it a super-superfood?

- **Hands-On Time: 5 minutes**
- **Cook Time: 20 minutes**

Serves 4

1 cup quinoa
1¼ cups water
1½ cups whole milk, divided
2 tablespoons unsalted butter
1 teaspoon unsweetened cocoa
1 tablespoon light brown sugar
½ teaspoon salt
2 tablespoons semisweet chocolate chips
2 medium bananas, diced
¼ cup chopped pecans

Stove Top

2C
2½
3C
4T
2t
2T
1t
2T
¼C

Doubled for stove top.

1. Add quinoa, water, ½ cup milk, butter, cocoa, sugar, and salt to the Instant Pot®. Stir well. Lock lid.

2. Press the Porridge button and cook for the default time of 20 minutes. When timer beeps, quick-release pressure until float valve drops and then unlock lid.

3. Transfer quinoa to a serving dish and fluff with a fork. Add chocolate chips and toss three times. Garnish with diced bananas and chopped pecans. Pour remaining 1 cup of milk over quinoa. Serve immediately.

Cinnamon Apple Crumb Muffins

Add a crumb topping to just about anything, and it becomes an instant hit. Add it to the classic combination of cinnamon and apples, and you have a grand slam on your hands. These muffins are a great treat for the family to wake up to as the weather cools. Serve with a slice or two of bacon and a warm cup of tea to round out this wintry, gluten-free comfort food.

- **Hands-On Time: 10 minutes**
- **Cook Time: 9 minutes**

Serves 6

Muffins

- 1¼ cups gluten-free all-purpose flour
- 2 teaspoons gluten-free baking powder
- ½ teaspoon baking soda
- 1 teaspoon ground cinnamon
- ⅛ teaspoon salt
- ½ teaspoon vanilla extract
- 3 tablespoons unsalted butter, melted
- 2 large eggs
- ¼ cup granulated sugar
- ¼ cup grated, peeled red apple
- 1 cup water

Crumb Topping

- 2 tablespoons gluten-free all-purpose flour
- ¼ cup light brown sugar
- ⅛ teaspoon ground cinnamon
- ⅛ teaspoon salt
- 2 tablespoons unsalted butter, softened

1. In a large bowl, combine flour, baking powder, baking soda, cinnamon, and salt.

2. In a medium bowl, combine vanilla, butter, eggs, sugar, and apple.

3. Pour wet ingredients from medium bowl to large bowl with dry ingredients. Gently combine ingredients. Do not overmix. Spoon mixture into six silicone cupcake liners lightly greased with either oil or cooking spray.

4. In a small bowl, combine crumb topping ingredients with a fork, pressing the butter into the dry ingredients until a crumbly mixture forms. Evenly distribute this among the cupcakes, sprinkling the mixture on top.

5. Add water to the Instant Pot® and insert steam rack. Place cupcake liners on top. Lock lid.

6. Press the Manual or Pressure Cook button and adjust cook time to 9 minutes. When timer beeps, quick-release pressure until float valve drops and then unlock lid.

7. Remove muffins from pot and set aside to cool 5 minutes before serving.

Banana Bread Corn Muffins

Putting a little twist on Grandma's classic banana bread, the cornmeal adds a little sweetness and rustic charm to this on-the-go breakfast. For an extra special something, add ¼ cup of nuts, raisins, or berries to up the fiber content as well as the nutritional value. If adding fresh blueberries, toss them in a little gluten-free flour prior to adding them to the batter to keep them from sinking to the bottom.

- **Hands-On Time: 10 minutes**
- **Cook Time: 9 minutes**

Serves 6

¾ cup gluten-free all-purpose flour

½ cup self-rising cornmeal

2 tablespoons granulated sugar

2 teaspoons gluten-free baking powder

½ teaspoon baking soda

⅛ teaspoon salt

½ teaspoon vanilla extract

3 tablespoons unsalted butter, melted

2 large eggs

2 ripe medium bananas, mashed with fork

1 cup water

1 In a large bowl, combine flour, cornmeal, sugar, baking powder, baking soda, and salt.

2 In a medium bowl, combine vanilla, butter, eggs, and bananas.

3 Add wet ingredients from medium bowl to large bowl with dry ingredients. Gently combine ingredients. Do not overmix. Spoon mixture into six silicone cupcake liners lightly greased with either oil or cooking spray.

4 Add water to the Instant Pot® and insert steam rack. Carefully place muffin cups in steamer basket. Lock lid.

5 Press the Manual or Pressure Cook button and adjust cook time to 9 minutes. When timer beeps, quick-release pressure until float valve drops and then unlock lid.

6 Remove muffins from pot and set aside to cool 5 minutes before serving.

Trail Mix Muffins

A quick gluten-free breakfast doesn't have to be unhealthy. Hit the road with these delicious and nutritious on-the-go muffins. Switch this recipe up by using your favorite chopped nuts or swapping out the peanut butter chips for chocolate chips. You can also add dried cherries instead of raisins, or swap out the sunflower seeds for pepitas! The possibilities are endless, so tailor this special recipe to your personal taste.

- **Hands-On Time: 10 minutes**
- **Cook Time: 9 minutes**

Serves 6

¾ cup gluten-free all-purpose flour
¼ cup old-fashioned oats
¼ cup raisins
2 tablespoons chopped pecans
1 tablespoon salted sunflower seeds
1 tablespoon peanut butter chips
¼ cup granulated sugar
2 teaspoons gluten-free baking powder
½ teaspoon baking soda
¼ teaspoon ground cinnamon
⅛ teaspoon salt
1 teaspoon vanilla extract
4 tablespoons unsalted butter, melted and cooled
2 large eggs, whisked
1 cup water

1 In a large bowl, combine flour, oats, raisins, pecans, sunflower seeds, peanut butter chips, sugar, baking powder, baking soda, cinnamon, and salt.

2 In a medium bowl, combine vanilla, butter, and eggs.

3 Add wet ingredients from medium bowl to large bowl with dry ingredients. Gently combine ingredients. Do not overmix. Spoon mixture into six silicone cupcake liners lightly greased with either oil or cooking spray.

4 Add water to the Instant Pot® and insert steam rack. Carefully place muffin cups in steamer basket. Lock lid.

5 Press the Manual or Pressure Cook button and adjust cook time to 9 minutes. When timer beeps, quick-release pressure until float valve drops and then unlock lid.

6 Remove muffins from pot and set aside to cool 5 minutes before serving.

Cinnamon Roll–French Toast Casserole

Once this casserole starts cooking and the sweet aroma wafts through the house, your family members will think that they are in the food court at the mall, approaching that very popular, yet gluten-filled, cinnamon roll maker! There's no reason you should feel left out anymore: make your own casserole brimming with all off the same delicious flavors!

- **Hands-On Time: 10 minutes**
- **Cook Time: 25 minutes**

Serves 4

Casserole
4 cups cubed gluten-free bread, dried out overnight
2 cups whole milk
3 large eggs
1 teaspoon vanilla extract
2 tablespoons pure maple syrup
1 teaspoon ground cinnamon
⅛ teaspoon salt
¼ cup raisins
2 tablespoons chopped pecans
2 tablespoons unsalted butter, melted and cooled
1 cup water

Cream Cheese Drizzle
1 tablespoon whole milk
1 tablespoon powdered sugar
2 tablespoons cream cheese

1　Add bread to a 7-cup glass dish greased with either oil or cooking spray. Set aside.

2　In a medium bowl, whisk together milk, eggs, vanilla, maple syrup, cinnamon, and salt. Pour over bread in glass dish. Evenly scatter raisins and pecans over bread and evenly drizzle butter over the top.

3　Add water to the Instant Pot®. Insert steam rack. Place glass dish on top of steam rack. Lock lid.

4　Press the Manual or Pressure Cook button and adjust cook time to 25 minutes. When timer beeps, quick-release pressure until float valve drops and then unlock lid.

5　Remove glass bowl from the Instant Pot®. Transfer to a rack and cool 10 minutes.

6　Combine milk, sugar, and cream cheese in a small bowl. Drizzle over casserole. Spoon casserole into four bowls and serve.

Chocolate Hazelnut–French Toast Casserole

That very popular brand of chocolate hazelnut spread takes this French toast casserole to the next level. A marriage made in heaven, chocolate and hazelnut not only taste like a dream; they also contain fiber, iron, and calcium to help you on your healthy, gluten-free journey. Try this quick casserole for breakfast or even as a dessert!

- **Hands-On Time: 10 minutes**
- **Cook Time: 25 minutes**

Serves 4

4 cups cubed gluten-free bread, dried out overnight

4 tablespoons chocolate hazelnut spread

2 cups whole milk

3 large eggs

1 teaspoon vanilla extract

2 tablespoons granulated sugar

⅛ teaspoon salt

3 tablespoons unsalted butter, cut into 6 pats

1 cup water

2 tablespoons powdered sugar

1 Add bread to a 7-cup glass dish greased with either oil or cooking spray. Set aside.

2 In a medium bowl, whisk together chocolate hazelnut spread, milk, eggs, vanilla, sugar, and salt. Pour over bread in glass dish. Place pats of butter on top.

3 Add water to the Instant Pot®. Insert steam rack. Place glass dish on steam rack. Lock lid.

4 Press the Manual or Pressure Cook button and adjust cook time to 25 minutes. When timer beeps, quick-release pressure until float valve drops and then unlock lid.

5 Remove glass bowl from the Instant Pot®. Transfer to a rack and cool 10 minutes.

6 Garnish casserole with powdered sugar and serve.

Zucchini Nut Bread

This recipe is essential when your garden is overgrown with zucchini. Zucchini bread has a similar taste to banana bread, so your picky eaters will never know the difference. And when you concentrate on what you can eat versus what you can't eat while on a gluten-free diet, you'll realize that the options and variety are quite broad!

- **Hands-On Time: 10 minutes**
- **Cook Time: 30 minutes**

Serves 6

2 large eggs

4 tablespoons whole milk

4 tablespoons unsalted butter, melted and cooled

½ cup grated zucchini (approximately 1 medium)

1⅓ cups gluten-free all-purpose flour

1½ teaspoons gluten-free baking powder

½ teaspoon baking soda

½ cup granulated sugar

½ teaspoon ground cinnamon

⅛ teaspoon salt

¼ cup chopped pecans

1 cup water

1 Lightly grease a 7" springform pan with either oil or cooking spray and set aside.

2 In a medium bowl, whisk together eggs, milk, and butter. Stir in zucchini.

3 In a large bowl, combine flour, baking powder, baking soda, sugar, cinnamon, and salt.

4 Add wet ingredients from medium bowl to large bowl with dry ingredients. Stir until combined. Fold in pecans. Do not overmix, as some lumps are fine.

5 Transfer mixture to greased springform pan.

6 Add water to the Instant Pot® and insert steam rack. Place springform pan on top. Lock lid.

7 Press the Manual or Pressure Cook button and adjust cook time to 30 minutes. When timer beeps, quick-release pressure until float valve drops and then unlock lid.

8 Unlock springform pan and let cool 10 minutes. Slice and serve.

Creamed Corn Buttermilk Corn Bread

Have you ever bitten into a piece of corn bread that was so dry you decided you didn't like corn bread? Well, try again. The addition of the creamed corn and onion lends a moisture to this bread that will have you coming back for more. The steam cooking of the Instant Pot® helps keep the moisture in as well, making this an excellent gluten-free side to a hearty stew or chili.

- **Hands-On Time: 10 minutes**
- **Cook Time: 30 minutes**

Serves 4

1 large egg
1½ cups self-rising buttermilk cornmeal mix
½ cup creamed corn
⅓ cup peeled and diced sweet onion
½ cup whole milk
1 tablespoon unsalted butter, melted
½ teaspoon granulated sugar
⅛ teaspoon salt
⅛ teaspoon ground pepper
1 cup water

1 Lightly grease a 7" springform pan with either oil or cooking spray and set aside.

2 In a large bowl, combine egg, cornmeal, creamed corn, onion, milk, butter, sugar, salt, and pepper.

3 Transfer mixture to greased springform pan.

4 Add water to the Instant Pot® and insert steam rack. Place springform pan on top. Lock lid.

5 Press the Manual or Pressure Cook button and adjust cook time to 30 minutes. When timer beeps, quick-release pressure until float valve drops and then unlock lid.

6 Unlock springform pan and slice corn bread. Serve.

Homemade Mixed-Berry Breakfast Syrup

The homemade version of this syrup ensures that there are no processed ingredients, so you don't have to wonder if there is any hidden gluten. You can use this recipe with whatever frozen berries or citrus fruits you have on hand. Orange juice and orange zest are especially nice with the mixed berries. You can also try lime juice and lime zest with a sweet cherry syrup for a change!

- **Hands-On Time: 5 minutes**
- **Cook Time: 3 minutes**

Yields 1 cup

1 pound frozen mixed berries
1 tablespoon unsalted butter
½ cup pure maple syrup
¼ cup freshly squeezed
   orange juice
1 tablespoon orange zest
¼ teaspoon vanilla extract
⅛ teaspoon salt

1. Add all ingredients to the Instant Pot®. Lock lid.

2. Press the Manual or Pressure Cook button and adjust cook time to 3 minutes. When timer beeps, quick-release pressure until float valve drops and then unlock lid.

3. Transfer ingredients to a food processor or blender and pulse until desired consistency. Serve warm or cool.

3

Soups, Stews, and Chilis

Why take the time to make a homemade soup when there are so many canned varieties available? Well, there are two very good reasons. The first is that homemade soup tastes better, as you are cooking with fresh ingredients, and each meal can be tailored to individual preferences. Second, it can be challenging to find canned soups that are 100 percent gluten-free, as there are so many hidden sources of gluten lingering in even the best-intended "healthy" products.

Traditionally, you've needed low heat and a long cooking time to marry together all of the wonderful spices and flavors that make any soup great, but not anymore. The pressurized heat in your Instant Pot® can save the day. Although there is a Slow Cook button on your Instant Pot® you can use when time isn't an issue, cooking at high pressure can allow you to serve a finished dinner within an hour. To cut back on time even more, you can find precut onions and peppers in the freezer section of your local grocery store that work great in a pinch. From Spicy Tex-Mex Chili to Roasted Red Pepper and Tomato Bisque, to Veggie Orzo Soup and Bean and Ham Soup, there's something for everyone! So, break out your ladle, because dinner is almost ready.

Chicken Broth

Many commercially produced broths contain wheat, so making a homemade version ensures that your cooking is gluten-free. After making a whole chicken in the Instant Pot® or picking up a precooked bird at the supermarket, don't forget to make the broth. Along with the carcass, you would be throwing away excellent nutrients and minerals, as well as a supertasty and simple broth for your next soup meal.

- **Hands-On Time: 10 minutes**
- **Cook Time: 30 minutes**

Yields 6 cups

1 chicken carcass from a whole chicken

2 large carrots, peeled and cut into chunks

2 stalks celery, cut into chunks

1 small yellow onion, peeled and chopped

1 bay leaf

2 cloves garlic, peeled and halved

½ teaspoon apple cider vinegar

1 teaspoon salt

6 cups water

1 Place all ingredients in the Instant Pot®. Lock lid.

2 Press the Manual or Pressure Cook button and adjust cook time to 30 minutes. When timer beeps, let pressure release naturally until float valve drops and then unlock lid.

3 Use a slotted spoon to remove and discard solids from the broth. Strain the remaining liquid through a fine-mesh sieve or cheese-cloth. Refrigerate broth up to 4 days or freeze up to 6 months.

IS STORE-BOUGHT BROTH GLUTEN-FREE?

You might think that there is no gluten in canned broths; however, many commercial broths, including bouillon, do contain wheat. Be careful to read labels when you're buying broth off the shelves.

Vegetable Broth

Broth is the very foundation of any soup, so making your own fresh broth adds so much dimension to your next meal, and there is none of the hidden wheat that is often found in store-bought broth. The recipe here is merely a guideline. Through the week, save those celery leaves, broccoli stems, and extra parsnips. "One man's trash is another man's treasure" never rang so true, as these seemingly throw-away pieces lend tremendous flavor to your next broth.

- **Hands-On Time: 10 minutes**
- **Cook Time: 30 minutes**

Yields 6 cups

3 large carrots, peeled and cut into chunks

2 stalks celery, cut into chunks

1 small yellow onion, peeled and chopped

1 medium potato, peeled and chopped

1 bay leaf

2 cloves garlic, peeled and halved

1 tablespoon tamari

½ teaspoon salt

6 cups water

1 Place all ingredients in the Instant Pot®. Lock lid.

2 Press the Manual or Pressure Cook button and adjust cook time to 30 minutes. When timer beeps, let pressure release naturally until float valve drops and then unlock lid.

3 Use a slotted spoon to remove and discard solids from the broth. Strain the remaining liquid through a fine-mesh sieve or cheesecloth. Refrigerate broth up to 4 days or freeze up to 6 months.

Beef Broth

For many people with gluten allergies, gut health is a primary concern. Bone broth has many healing benefits, including to the digestive tract. Beef soup bones can be bought at most supermarkets and butcher shops. If they are not on display, don't hesitate to ask. Making your own beef and bone broth is very popular these days, so asking for bones won't seem weird. You can also use oxtail or neck bones as a substitute.

- **Hands-On Time: 10 minutes**
- **Cook Time: 30 minutes**

Yields 6 cups

3 pounds beef soup bones

2 large carrots, peeled and cut into chunks

2 stalks celery, cut into chunks

1 small yellow onion, peeled and chopped

1 bay leaf

2 cloves garlic, peeled and halved

½ teaspoon apple cider vinegar

1 teaspoon salt

6 cups water

1 Place all ingredients in the Instant Pot®. Lock lid.

2 Press the Manual or Pressure Cook button and adjust cook time to 30 minutes. When timer beeps, let pressure release naturally until float valve drops and then unlock lid.

3 Use a slotted spoon to remove and discard solids from the broth. Strain the remaining liquid through a fine-mesh sieve or cheesecloth. Refrigerate broth up to 4 days or freeze up to 6 months.

Three-Bean Chili

So, a gluten-free gal, a clean-eating guy, and a vegan walk into a bar...what do you feed them? Three-Bean Chili, of course! This warm and nourishing bowl of chili will have folks on all diets licking their flavor-filled and nutrient-rich bowls. Beans are naturally gluten-free, but read those labels, as some brands may contain additives such as wheat starch or wheat flour.

- **Hands-On Time: 10 minutes**
- **Cook Time: 41 minutes**

Serves 4

1 tablespoon olive oil

1 small red onion, peeled and diced

1 medium green bell pepper, seeded and diced

1 large carrot, peeled and diced

4 cloves garlic, peeled and minced

1 (15-ounce) can kidney beans, drained and rinsed

1 (15-ounce) can cannellini beans, drained and rinsed

1 (15-ounce) can black beans, drained and rinsed

2 tablespoons chili powder

1 teaspoon ground cumin

1 small jalapeño, seeded and diced

1 teaspoon salt

1 (28-ounce) can diced tomatoes, including juice

¼ cup vegetable broth

1 Press the Sauté button on the Instant Pot®. Heat oil 30 seconds. Add the onion, bell pepper, and carrot. Stir-fry 5 minutes until onions are translucent. Add garlic and heat for an additional minute.

2 Add remaining ingredients to pot and stir to combine. Lock lid.

3 Press the Meat button and cook for default time of 35 minutes. When timer beeps, let pressure release naturally until float valve drops and then unlock lid.

4 Ladle chili into four bowls and serve warm.

Spicy Tex-Mex Chili

Based on my experience, you will never please all of the chili purists out there. And, by the way, each chili purist alive has his or her very own unique idea of what chili is. So, cater to your own taste buds and experiment with different types of recipes. It is like comparing apples to oranges when deciding on meat or not, beans or not, the level of heat, and even the amount of liquid. In this Tex-Mex version, the fat from the pork plays so well with the tasty combination of corn and black beans. And, if you want to top this with a few Fritos, go for it!

- **Hands-On Time: 15 minutes**
- **Cook Time: 44 minutes**

Serves 4

1 tablespoon olive oil

1 small yellow onion, peeled and diced

1 medium red bell pepper, seeded and diced

2 stalks celery, chopped

½ pound ground pork

4 cloves garlic, peeled and minced

1 cup sliced white mushrooms

1 (15.5-ounce) can corn, drained

1 (15-ounce) can black beans, drained and rinsed

2 tablespoons chili powder

1 teaspoon smoked paprika

2 chipotles in adobo sauce, finely diced

1 teaspoon adobo sauce

1 teaspoon salt

1 (28-ounce) can diced tomatoes, including juice

¼ cup beef broth

1 cup shredded Cheddar cheese

1 Press the Sauté button on the Instant Pot®. Heat oil 30 seconds. Add onion, bell pepper, and celery to pot. Stir-fry 3 minutes until onions are tender. Add pork and heat 5 minutes until pork is no longer pink. Add garlic and heat for an additional minute.

2 Add remaining ingredients, except cheese, to pot and stir to combine. Lock lid.

3 Press the Meat button and cook for default time of 35 minutes. When timer beeps, let pressure release naturally until float valve drops and then unlock lid.

4 Ladle chili into four bowls and garnish with cheese. Serve warm.

Chicken and Green Chile Chili

This is one of those healthy dishes that you make for yourself but that gets eaten by your family, leaving no leftovers for that dreamy lunch the next day. Garnish with crushed gluten-free tortilla chips for some added texture to this lovely dinner. And don't forget your glass of white wine, which is a perfect pairing to this warm meal.

- **Hands-On Time: 10 minutes**
- **Cook Time: 21 minutes**

Serves 4

1 tablespoon olive oil

1 pound ground chicken

1 medium yellow onion, peeled and diced

1 stalk celery, diced

3 cloves garlic, peeled and minced

1 cup chicken broth

1 (28-ounce) can diced tomatoes, including liquid

1 (14.5-ounce) can great northern beans, rinsed and drained

2 (4-ounce) cans diced green chiles, including liquid

1 teaspoon salt

1 tablespoon chili powder

1 tablespoon fresh thyme leaves

1 cup sour cream

1 Press the Sauté button on the Instant Pot® and heat oil 30 seconds. Add chicken, onion, and celery to pot. Stir-fry 5 minutes until chicken is no longer pink. Add garlic and cook for an additional minute.

2 Stir in remaining ingredients except for sour cream. Lock lid.

3 Press the Manual or Pressure Cook button and adjust cook time to 15 minutes. When timer beeps, let pressure release naturally until float valve drops and then unlock lid. Stir in sour cream.

4 Ladle chili into four bowls and serve warm.

Roasted Red Pepper and Tomato Bisque

When choosing tomatoes for this soup, get ones that are very ripe, as the natural sugars and brightness of the soup will be enhanced. If tomatoes are out of season, use a 28-ounce can of whole tomatoes with juice, decrease the chicken broth to 3 cups, and follow the recipe accordingly.

- **Hands-On Time: 10 minutes**
- **Cook Time: 15 minutes**

Serves 4

1 tablespoon olive oil

2 teaspoons balsamic vinegar

1 small sweet onion, peeled and diced

1 stalk celery, thinly chopped

8 medium tomatoes, seeded and quartered

1 (12-ounce) jar roasted red peppers, drained and diced

4 cups chicken broth

1 tablespoon cooking sherry

½ cup julienned fresh basil leaves, divided

1 teaspoon salt

1 teaspoon ground black pepper

1 cup whole milk

1 Press the Sauté button on the Instant Pot® and heat oil and balsamic vinegar 30 seconds. Add onion and celery to pot. Sauté 5 minutes until onions are translucent. Add tomatoes and sauté 3 minutes until tomatoes start to break down.

2 Add roasted red peppers, broth, sherry, ¼ cup basil, salt, and pepper to pot. Lock lid.

3 Press the Manual or Pressure Cook button and adjust cook time to 7 minutes. When timer beeps, quick-release pressure until float valve drops and then unlock lid.

4 Add milk to pot. Use an immersion blender to purée the bisque in pot or use a stand blender to purée the bisque in batches.

5 Ladle bisque into four bowls and garnish with remaining basil. Serve warm.

Cheeseburger Soup

From the beef to the pickles, this Cheeseburger Soup hits all the flavors of your favorite burger. So, skip the bun, the processed ingredients, and the wasted money on fast food, and make this recipe your new gluten-free family favorite. And don't skip that pickle garnish—it makes the soup!

- **Hands-On Time: 10 minutes**
- **Cook Time: 16 minutes**

Serves 4

1 tablespoon olive oil

1 pound ground beef

1 medium yellow onion, peeled and diced

1 small green bell pepper, seeded and diced

1 medium carrot, peeled and shredded

1 (15-ounce) can diced tomatoes, including juice

2 teaspoons yellow mustard

1 teaspoon smoked paprika

1 teaspoon garlic powder

½ teaspoon salt

4 cups beef broth

2 cups shredded iceberg lettuce

1 cup shredded Cheddar cheese, divided

½ cup diced dill pickles

1 Press the Sauté button on the Instant Pot® and heat the oil 30 seconds. Add beef, onion, and green pepper to the pot. Sauté 5 minutes until beef begins to brown. Add carrot and heat for an additional minute.

2 Add tomatoes with juice, mustard, paprika, garlic powder, salt, and beef broth to pot. Lock lid.

3 Press the Manual or Pressure Cook button and adjust cook time to 7 minutes. When timer beeps, quick-release pressure until float valve drops and then unlock lid.

4 Stir in lettuce and ½ cup cheese and simmer 3 minutes.

5 Ladle soup into four bowls and garnish with diced dill pickles and remaining cheese. Serve warm.

Meatball Soup

Mamma mia—that's a spicy gluten-free meatball! Well, it depends on your taste buds. There is cayenne in the actual meatball and red pepper flakes in the soup. If you like it spicy, proceed as stated. If you like it less spicy, eliminate the cayenne. If spice isn't your thing, you can take out both. This is your meal!

- **Hands-On Time: 15 minutes**
- **Cook Time: 18 minutes**

Serves 4

Meatballs
- ½ pound ground pork
- 2 tablespoons gluten-free bread crumbs
- 2 tablespoons grated Parmesan cheese
- 1 tablespoon Italian seasoning
- ½ teaspoon cayenne pepper
- ½ teaspoon salt
- 1 large egg, whisked
- 2 cloves garlic, peeled and minced
- 2 tablespoons olive oil, divided

Soup
- 1 tablespoon olive oil
- 1 small red onion, peeled and diced
- 1 medium carrot, peeled and shredded
- 1 Russet potato, scrubbed and small-diced
- 1 (15-ounce) can diced fire-roasted tomatoes, including juice
- 4 cups beef broth
- ½ teaspoon salt
- ½ teaspoon ground black pepper
- ¼ teaspoon red pepper flakes
- ½ cup chopped fresh basil leaves

1. In a medium bowl, combine ground pork, bread crumbs, Parmesan cheese, Italian seasoning, cayenne pepper, salt, egg, and garlic. Form the mixture into twenty-four meatballs.

2. Press the Sauté button on the Instant Pot® and heat 1 tablespoon oil 30 seconds. Add half the meatballs to pot and sear 3 minutes, turning them to brown all sides. Remove the first batch and set aside. Add the remaining oil and repeat with the remaining meatballs. Remove the meatballs from pot. Meatballs will not be completely cooked, as they will finish in the soup.

3. Press the Sauté button on the Instant Pot® and heat the oil 30 seconds. Add onion, carrot, and potato; sauté 5 minutes until onions become translucent.

4. Add meatballs to pot along with tomatoes with juice, broth, salt, black pepper, red pepper flakes, and basil. Lock lid.

5. Press the Manual or Pressure Cook button and adjust cook time to 7 minutes. When timer beeps, quick-release pressure until float valve drops and then unlock lid.

6. Ladle soup into four bowls. Serve warm.

Bean and Ham Soup

Smoky and hearty, this soup is perfect for whatever ails you. Making soup from scratch with dried beans traditionally takes hours, including presoaking the beans and cooking the soup. It will take under an hour to make this dish in your Instant Pot®.

- **Hands-On Time: 5 minutes**
- **Cook Time: 45 minutes**

Serves 4

½ pound dried great northern beans, rinsed

4 cups chicken broth

1 (8-ounce) can tomato sauce

1 small yellow onion, peeled and diced

1 large carrot, peeled and diced

2 stalks celery, chopped

4 cloves garlic, peeled and minced

½ teaspoon salt

1 ham hock

1 bay leaf

4 tablespoons fresh thyme leaves

1 Add all ingredients to the Instant Pot® and stir to combine. Lock lid.

2 Press the Manual or Pressure Cook button and adjust cook time to 45 minutes. When timer beeps, let pressure release naturally until float valve drops and then unlock lid.

3 Discard bay leaf. Using two forks, shred meat off of ham bone. Discard bone.

4 Ladle soup into four bowls and serve warm.

Split Pea Soup

This one-pot meal of creamy soup will warm up your insides and spirit during the winter months, not to mention the limited dishes you'll have to wash! Pair it with a grilled Gruyère cheese sandwich on gluten-free bread for a nice twist or round it out with a light Merlot by the fireplace with the one you love.

- **Hands-On Time: 15 minutes**
- **Cook Time: 21 minutes**

Serves 4

3 tablespoons unsalted butter

3 large carrots, peeled and diced

2 stalks celery, diced

1 small yellow onion, peeled and diced

1 ham hock

1 pound dried split green peas, rinsed

4 cups chicken broth

2 cups water

1 tablespoon cooking sherry

1 tablespoon dried thyme leaves

1 teaspoon salt

1 teaspoon ground black pepper

1 bay leaf

4 tablespoons sour cream

1 Press the Sauté button on the Instant Pot® and heat butter 30 seconds until melted. Add carrot, celery, and onion to pot. Sauté 5 minutes until onions are translucent. Add ham hock and rinsed peas and cook for an additional minute.

2 Add broth, water, sherry, thyme, salt, pepper, and bay leaf to pot. Lock lid.

3 Press the Manual or Pressure Cook button and adjust cook time to 15 minutes. When timer beeps, let pressure release naturally for 10 minutes. Manually release any additional pressure and unlock lid.

4 Discard bay leaf. Using two forks, shred meat off of ham bone. Discard bone.

5 Ladle soup into four bowls and garnish with sour cream. Serve warm.

GREEN OR YELLOW SPLIT PEAS

The green and yellow split pea are similar in size, taste, and texture, and there is hardly a difference between them. Although the consensus is that the yellow peas are slighter milder than the sweeter green variety, these two nutritious legumes are interchangeable in recipes.

Loaded Broccoli and Bacon Soup

This smooth and cheesy broccoli soup is enhanced with the smoky and crunchy bacon and velvety sour cream. This gluten-free soup is a wonderful comfort meal after a brisk run on a cool fall evening or after a family snowball fight on a cold winter's day.

- **Hands-On Time: 15 minutes**
- **Cook Time: 30 minutes**

Serves 4

2 teaspoons unsalted butter

6 slices bacon, diced

1 medium sweet onion, peeled and diced

1 large carrot, peeled and diced

1 small russet potato, scrubbed and diced

1 pound fresh broccoli, chopped

¼ cup grated Cheddar cheese

1 tablespoon Dijon mustard

1 teaspoon salt

1 teaspoon ground black pepper

4 cups chicken broth

¼ cup whole milk

4 tablespoons sour cream

1 Press the Sauté button on the Instant Pot® and heat butter 30 seconds until melted. Add bacon to pot and cook 5 minutes until crispy. Set bacon aside 5 minutes on a plate lined with paper towels. Crumble bacon when cooled. Add onion, carrot, and potato to pot. Sauté 5 minutes until the onions are translucent.

2 Add broccoli, cheese, mustard, salt, pepper, and broth to the Instant Pot®. Lock lid.

3 Press the Soup button and adjust cook time to 20 minutes. When timer beeps, quick-release pressure until float valve drops and then unlock lid.

4 Add milk to pot. Use an immersion blender to blend the soup in pot until desired smoothness or use a stand blender to blend the soup in batches.

5 Ladle soup into four bowls and garnish with crumbled bacon and sour cream. Serve warm.

Potato and Leek Bisque

Traditionally, this style of soup doesn't use bacon. This version, however, calls for one slice, which is just enough to lend that smoky note that takes this recipe to the next level. With that said, if you are a traditionalist, just eliminate the bacon. Also, heavy cream or half-and-half can be used in lieu of the milk for a richer soup. The potatoes provide a good dose of healthy starch—something you may have thought could only be quelled by a slice of bread.

- **Hands-On Time: 10 minutes**
- **Cook Time: 25 minutes**

Serves 4

2 tablespoons unsalted butter

1 slice bacon, diced

3 leeks, trimmed, rinsed, and diced

6 cups diced Yukon Gold potatoes, cut into ½" cubes

4 cups chicken broth

1 teaspoon sriracha

2 teaspoons dried thyme leaves

½ teaspoon sea salt

¼ cup whole milk

1 Press the Sauté button on the Instant Pot®. Heat butter 30 seconds until melted. Add bacon and leeks to pot and stir-fry 5 minutes until fat is rendered and leeks become tender.

2 Add potatoes, broth, sriracha, thyme, and salt to pot and stir to combine. Lock lid.

3 Press the Manual or Pressure Cook button and cook for default time of 15 minutes. When timer beeps, let pressure release naturally for 5 minutes. Manually release any additional pressure until float valve drops and then unlock lid.

4 Add milk. Use an immersion blender to blend the soup in pot until desired consistency or use a stand blender to blend the soup in batches.

5 Ladle bisque into four bowls and serve warm.

Moroccan Lamb and Chickpea Soup

This beautifully seasoned soup will automatically put a stamp in your passport, transporting you to the beautiful and colorful spice markets of the streets of Morocco. The chickpeas provide your body with a good dose of fiber and carbohydrates sometimes missing in the gluten-free lifestyle.

- **Hands-On Time: 10 minutes**
- **Cook Time: 13 minutes**

Serves 4

1 tablespoon olive oil

1 pound ground lamb

1 medium red onion, peeled and diced

1 medium carrot, peeled and shredded

3 cloves garlic, peeled and minced

1 (15-ounce) can diced tomatoes, including juice

4 cups chicken broth

1 (15.5-ounce) can chickpeas, rinsed and drained

½ teaspoon turmeric

½ teaspoon ground ginger

¼ teaspoon ground cinnamon

½ teaspoon salt

½ cup chopped fresh cilantro

4 tablespoons plain full-fat Greek yogurt

1 Press the Sauté button on the Instant Pot® and heat oil 30 seconds. Add lamb and onion to pot. Sauté 5 minutes until lamb begins to brown. Add carrot and garlic and heat for an additional minute.

2 Add tomatoes with juice, broth, chickpeas, turmeric, ginger, cinnamon, and salt to pot. Lock lid.

3 Press the Manual or Pressure Cook button and adjust cook time to 7 minutes. When timer beeps, quick-release pressure until float valve drops and then unlock lid.

4 Ladle soup into four bowls and garnish with cilantro and yogurt. Serve warm.

ARE CHICKPEAS AND GARBANZO BEANS THE SAME?

Yes, these are the same legume and are interchangeable in recipes. Most American grocers will show both words on the label.

Classic Beef Stew

Forget the family table. Enjoy this incredibly satisfying and hearty stew in front of the fireplace on a cold winter's night. The steam and pressure from the Instant Pot® transform the beef cubes into a melt-in-your-mouth state, especially when surrounded by the fresh sauce and veggies. And, if you happen to have leftovers, this stew is even better the next day, especially if you have some gluten-free bread or corn bread to enjoy it with!

- **Hands-On Time: 15 minutes**
- **Cook Time: 46 minutes**

Serves 6

2 tablespoons olive oil

2 pounds beef stew cubes

1 medium sweet onion, peeled and diced

4 cloves garlic, peeled and minced

3 cups beef broth

½ cup dry red wine

1 (14.5-ounce) can crushed tomatoes, including juice

2 medium carrots, peeled and diced

1 stalk celery, chopped

2 medium russet potatoes, scrubbed and small-diced

1 teaspoon salt

½ teaspoon ground black pepper

2 tablespoons chopped fresh rosemary

2 tablespoons gluten-free all-purpose flour

4 tablespoons water

¼ cup chopped fresh Italian flat-leaf parsley

1. Press the Sauté button on the Instant Pot® and heat oil 30 seconds. Add beef and onion to pot. Stir-fry 5 minutes until beef is seared and onions are translucent. Add garlic and sauté for an additional minute.

2. Add beef broth and wine and deglaze pot by scraping up any bits from the sides and bottom of pot. Add tomatoes with juice, carrots, celery, potatoes, salt, pepper, and rosemary. Lock lid.

3. Press the Meat button and cook for the default time of 35 minutes. When timer beeps, let pressure release naturally until float valve drops and then unlock lid.

4. Create a slurry by whisking together flour and water in a small bowl. Add slurry to pot and let simmer 5 minutes, stirring occasionally.

5. Ladle stew into six bowls, garnish with parsley, and serve warm.

Jamaican Red Beans and Rice Soup

Oh, mon—this soup has layers of flavors that will dance on your tongue. If heat is an issue, the Scotch bonnet (or habanero pepper) is not your friend. Simply substitute ¼ teaspoon cayenne to give just enough heat to balance the flavors. And, as with all seasoning blends, read your labels to ensure that no anticlumping gluten fillers were added to your beautiful spice blends.

- **Hands-On Time: 10 minutes**
- **Cook Time: 50 minutes**

Serves 4

2 teaspoons olive oil

3 slices bacon, diced

5 green onions, sliced

2 large carrots, peeled and diced

1 stalk celery, chopped

1 Scotch bonnet or habanero pepper, seeded, veins removed, and minced

½ pound dried small red beans

1 (13.5-ounce) can coconut milk

2 cups chicken broth

1 (15-ounce) can diced tomatoes, including juice

1 tablespoon Jamaican jerk seasoning

1 teaspoon salt

4 cups cooked basmati rice

1 cup chopped fresh parsley

1 lime, quartered

1 Press the Sauté button on the Instant Pot® and heat oil 30 seconds. Add bacon, onion, carrot, celery, and Scotch bonnet to pot. Stir-fry 5 minutes until onions are translucent.

2 Add red beans, coconut milk, broth, tomatoes with juice, Jamaican jerk seasoning, and salt to pot and stir to combine. Lock lid.

3 Press the Manual or Pressure Cook button and adjust cook time to 45 minutes. When timer beeps, let pressure release naturally until float valve drops and then unlock lid.

4 Ladle soup into four bowls over cooked rice and garnish with parsley. Squeeze a quarter of lime over each bowl. Serve warm.

Veggie Orzo Soup

Although garnishing this dish with your basic Parmesan cheese will do the trick, try buying a brick of Parmesan or Parmigiano-Reggiano in the fancy section of your supermarket. Use a thicker grate (instead of the fine side) to top this soup. The cheese will hold up longer as you dive into this beautiful dish. And don't forget to buy the gluten-free orzo!

- **Hands-On Time: 15 minutes**
- **Cook Time: 10 minutes**

Serves 4

5 cups vegetable broth
2 stalks celery, diced
1 small carrot, peeled and diced
1 small yellow onion, peeled and diced
2 cloves garlic, peeled and minced
½ cup gluten-free orzo
1 (15-ounce) can diced tomatoes, including juice
1 medium potato, peeled and small-diced
1 medium zucchini, diced
2 teaspoons dried thyme leaves
2 teaspoons dried oregano leaves
1 teaspoon salt
1 teaspoon ground black pepper
3 cups fresh baby spinach
4 tablespoons grated Parmesan cheese

1 Add all ingredients except spinach and Parmesan cheese to the Instant Pot®. Lock lid.

2 Press the Manual or Pressure Cook button and adjust cook time to 10 minutes. When timer beeps, quick-release pressure until float valve drops and then unlock lid. Add spinach and stir gently until wilted.

3 Ladle soup into four bowls, garnish with Parmesan cheese, and serve warm.

WHAT IF ORZO IS UNAVAILABLE?

Orzo, also known as *risoni*, is simply a rice-shaped pasta. If you can't find orzo in the store or online, simply replace it with a short-grain white rice.

Cream of Crab Soup

This soup has all the flavors of the East Coast. Although there are cheaper varieties of crab, the lump crabmeat is so hearty and provides bigger bites of this sumptuous crustacean. Heavy cream pairs beautifully with the crab; however, milk can be used to take the calories down a notch. Also, try adding fresh corn kernels to this soup for variety.

- **Hands-On Time: 10 minutes**
- **Cook Time: 21 minutes**

Serves 4

4 tablespoons unsalted butter

1 cup chopped leeks, cleaned and rinsed

2 large carrots, peeled and diced

2 stalks celery, chopped

4 cloves garlic, peeled and minced

2 teaspoons Italian seasoning

1 teaspoon salt

5 cups vegetable broth

1 pound lump crabmeat, picked through for shells, divided

2 tablespoons cooking sherry

¼ cup heavy cream

2 tablespoons fresh thyme leaves

1 Press the Sauté button on the Instant Pot®. Heat butter 30 seconds. Add leek, carrot, and celery to pot. Stir-fry 5 minutes until leeks are translucent. Add garlic and heat for an additional minute.

2 Add Italian seasoning, salt, broth, and ½ pound of crabmeat to pot and stir to combine. Lock lid.

3 Press the Manual or Pressure Cook button and adjust cook time to 15 minutes. When timer beeps, let pressure release naturally until float valve drops and then unlock lid.

4 Use an immersion blender to blend the soup in pot until smooth or use a stand blender to blend the soup in batches. Whisk in remaining crab, sherry, and heavy cream.

5 Ladle soup into four bowls, garnish with thyme, and serve warm.

Salmon Chowder

Salmon is prevalent in the Northwest, so this chowder is the Northwest's nod to the traditional clam chowder in the Northeast. Just as creamy and just as rich, Salmon Chowder is a warm and satisfying restaurant-worthy meal rich in omega-3 fatty acids and vitamins, and is a great source of protein.

- **Hands-On Time: 15 minutes**
- **Cook Time: 16 minutes**

Serves 4

1 tablespoon unsalted butter

2 slices bacon, diced

2 shallots, peeled and diced

1 stalk celery, diced

2 cloves garlic, peeled and minced

2 cups diced Yukon Gold potatoes

2 cups chicken broth

1 pound boneless, skinless salmon fillet, cut in 1" cubes

2 ears of corn, kernels sliced from cob

1 (14.75-ounce) can creamed corn

1 tablespoon chopped fresh dill

1 teaspoon salt

1 teaspoon ground black pepper

1 cup whole milk

1 tablespoon cornstarch

1 Press the Sauté button on the Instant Pot®. Heat butter 30 seconds. Add bacon, shallot, and celery to pot. Stir-fry 5 minutes. Add garlic and heat for an additional minute.

2 Add potatoes, broth, salmon, corn kernels, creamed corn, dill, salt, and pepper to pot and stir to combine. Lock lid.

3 Press the Manual or Pressure Cook button and adjust cook time to 5 minutes. When timer beeps, let pressure release naturally until float valve drops and then unlock lid.

4 Whisk together milk and cornstarch in a small bowl. Add mixture to pot and simmer 5 minutes to allow chowder to thicken.

5 Ladle chowder into four bowls and serve warm.

Mediterranean Fish Stew

You'll feel like you are cruising the blue water of the Med on your personal yacht with the fresh and healthy flavors of this stew. Olive oil, garlic, tomatoes, and fish are just some of the ingredients that scream Mediterranean fresh flavors. If you want to kick it up a notch, use some fresh oregano and basil in lieu of the Italian seasoning.

- **Hands-On Time: 10 minutes**
- **Cook Time: 14 minutes**

Serves 4

1 tablespoon olive oil

1 small yellow onion, peeled and diced

1 stalk celery, diced

1 large carrot, peeled and diced

4 cloves garlic, peeled and minced

2 cups baby red potatoes, scrubbed and small-diced

1 (8-ounce) bottle of clam juice

1 (28-ounce) can diced tomatoes, including juice

2 cups water

1 tablespoon Italian seasoning

1 pound skinless cod, cut in 1" cubes

1 teaspoon salt

1 bay leaf

1 Press the Sauté button on the Instant Pot®. Heat oil 30 seconds. Add onion, celery, and carrot to pot. Stir-fry 5 minutes until onions are translucent. Add garlic and heat for an additional minute.

2 Add remaining ingredients to pot and stir to combine. Lock lid.

3 Press the Manual or Pressure Cook button and adjust cook time to 8 minutes. When timer beeps, let pressure release naturally until float valve drops and then unlock lid.

4 Ladle stew into four bowls and serve warm.

Appetizers, Snacks, and Sauces

Living within certain dietary requirements is never harder than when you are with a group of friends. Chips and breads are everywhere, not to mention the hidden gluten found in so many sauces. And, let's face it, sometimes it gets annoying to have to ask about every last ingredient in a meal or a quick bite at a party. But this doesn't have to be your fate. Bring a healthy gluten-free option to share. Or, better yet, throw your own party and show folks what they've been missing! Appetizers are a great way to bring a group of people together to enjoy a game or to hold your friends over until you serve a meal.

But who wants to be stuck in the kitchen all day? Let the Instant Pot® be your helpful sous chef. Quick, hot food in minutes? Now that's how you throw a party! With amazing gluten-free appetizers ranging from Chili Nachos and Mini Reuben Potato Skins, to Cocktail Pizza Meatballs and Chinese Chicken Wings, the only problem you'll have is deciding which ones to make. And after the appetizers have been devoured, make some of the rich sauces from this chapter, such as Green Enchilada Sauce or Italian Ragù Sauce, to ladle over baked chicken breasts or a gluten-free pasta entrée!

Chili Nachos

This appetizer is always a crowd-pleaser. And now those with gluten allergies can join in on the fun—just make sure you get the right chips. The tortilla chips need to be made from corn, either blue or yellow, instead of wheat. There are also chips made from sweet potatoes, rice, and even beans if you want some variety. And your imagination is the limit when it comes to toppings. Try diced avocado, guacamole, sour cream, jalapeño slices, or sliced black or green olives.

- **Hands-On Time: 15 minutes**
- **Cook Time: 45 minutes**

Serves 8

1 tablespoon olive oil

1 small red onion, peeled and diced

1 medium green bell pepper, seeded and diced

½ pound ground beef

¼ pound ground pork

1 tablespoon chili powder

1 teaspoon garlic powder

1 teaspoon ground cumin

1 teaspoon salt

1 (14.5-ounce) can diced tomatoes, including juice

1 (4-ounce) can chopped green chiles, including juice

4 ounces cream cheese

½ cup shredded Cheddar cheese

2 Roma tomatoes, seeded and diced

4 scallions, sliced

1 bag corn tortilla chips

1   Press the Sauté button on the Instant Pot®. Heat oil 30 seconds. Add onion and bell pepper to pot. Stir-fry 5 minutes until onions are translucent. Add beef and pork and cook for an additional 5 minutes, using a wooden spoon to chop and stir as the meat cooks.

2   Add chili powder, garlic powder, cumin, salt, tomatoes with juice, and chiles with juice to pot and stir to combine. Lock lid.

3   Press the Meat button and cook for default time of 35 minutes. When timer beeps, let pressure release naturally until float valve drops and then unlock lid. Stir in cream cheese until melted and evenly distributed.

4   Transfer chili mixture to a serving dish. Garnish with cheese, Roma tomatoes, and scallions. Serve warm with chips.

Twice-Baked Baby Potatoes

Twice-baked russet potatoes are typically a pleaser as a side dish, and this mini version holds all the flavors of its bigger sibling. But, as with most things, the miniature version is just cuter. And since we eat with our eyes first, these twice-baked baby potatoes will soon be a family favorite.

- **Hands-On Time: 15 minutes**
- **Cook Time: 19 minutes**

Serves 10

4 slices bacon, halved

2 pounds baby yellow potatoes (approximately 10), scrubbed

1 cup water

2 tablespoons unsalted butter

¼ cup sour cream

¼ cup grated Cheddar cheese

2 tablespoons whole milk

½ teaspoon salt

½ teaspoon ground black pepper

2 tablespoons chopped fresh chives

1 Use a fork to pierce each potato four times. Set aside.

2 Press the Sauté button on the Instant Pot® and add bacon to pot. Cook 4 minutes until bacon is crisp. Set aside, leaving rendered fat in pot.

3 Add potatoes to pot and sauté 3 minutes to absorb some of the bacon flavor. Add water. Lock lid.

4 Press Manual or Pressure Cook button and adjust cook time to 7 minutes. When timer beeps, quick-release pressure until float valve drops and then unlock lid.

5 Using a slotted spoon, transfer potatoes to a plate. Let cool 5 minutes until you can handle them.

6 Preheat oven to 350°F.

7 Cut potatoes in half lengthwise. Scoop out approximately half of the potato, creating a boat. Add scooped-out potato to a medium bowl. Place potato halves on a baking sheet lined with parchment paper.

8 In medium bowl with scooped-out potatoes, add butter, sour cream, Cheddar cheese, milk, salt, and pepper. Combine until ingredients are well distributed. Spoon mixture into potato halves.

9 Bake potatoes for 5 minutes. While potatoes are baking, crumble bacon.

10 Remove potatoes from oven and transfer to a serving dish. Garnish with bacon and chives. Serve warm.

Cocktail Pizza Meatballs

These melt-in-your-mouth gooey mozzarella pizza meatballs will make you the best host in town. I mean, who doesn't like pizza? Especially when all of that flavor is rolled into a meatball covered in marinara? This is your new best appetizer, and your starch-loving friends will never know that it's gluten-free.

- **Hands-On Time: 15 minutes**
- **Cook Time: 28 minutes**

Yields 20 meatballs

- ¾ **pound ground beef**
- ½ **cup finely chopped pepperoni**
- 2 **large eggs**
- 1 **tablespoon Italian seasoning**
- 2 **cloves garlic, peeled and minced**
- ½ **cup gluten-free bread crumbs**
- 20 **mini mozzarella balls, known as** *ciliegine*
- 3 **tablespoons olive oil, divided**
- 2 **cups marinara sauce**
- 2 **cups water**
- 20 **fresh basil leaves**

1. In a medium bowl, combine beef, pepperoni, eggs, Italian seasoning, garlic, and bread crumbs. Form mixture into twenty meatballs. Press one mozzarella ball into the middle of each meatball, ensuring that meat completely surrounds mozzarella ball.

2. Press the Sauté button on the Instant Pot®. Heat 2 tablespoons oil 30 seconds. Place ten meatballs around the edge of pot. Sear meatballs 4 minutes, making sure to get each side. Remove meatballs from the Instant Pot® and set aside. Add the third tablespoon of oil and sear remaining meatballs 4 minutes. Remove meatballs from the Instant Pot® and set aside.

3. Discard extra juice and oil from the Instant Pot®. Add seared meatballs to a 7-cup glass dish. Pour marinara sauce over meatballs.

4. Add water to the Instant Pot®. Insert steam rack. Place the glass dish on top of the steam rack. Lock lid.

5. Press the Manual or Pressure Cook button and adjust cook time to 20 minutes. When timer beeps, let pressure release naturally for 10 minutes. Quick-release any additional pressure until float valve drops and then unlock lid.

6. Remove dish from the Instant Pot®. Garnish meatballs with fresh basil leaves. Serve with toothpicks so guests can easily retrieve meatballs.

Crab and Zucchini Dip

Add crab to any dish, and it ups the fancy meter; however, this dip couldn't be any easier to make. And because zucchini takes on the flavors surrounding it, this five-star dish will yield a healthy punch of fiber and nutrients while still delivering on flavor. Serve with gluten-free bread, corn chips, crudités, or some combination of the three.

- **Hands-On Time: 10 minutes**
- **Cook Time: 13 minutes**

Serves 8

⅔ **cup grated zucchini (approximately 1 medium)**

8 **ounces cream cheese, room temperature**

12 **ounces lump crabmeat, drained and picked over for shells**

⅓ **cup peeled and diced sweet onion**

½ **teaspoon lemon juice**

⅛ **teaspoon Worcestershire sauce**

2 **teaspoons prepared horseradish**

¼ **teaspoon smoked paprika**

¼ **teaspoon cayenne pepper**

1 **teaspoon salt**

¼ **teaspoon ground black pepper**

1 **cup water**

¼ **cup grated Parmesan cheese**

1 Squeeze grated zucchini in paper towels to extract excess moisture.

2 In a medium bowl, combine zucchini, cream cheese, crab, onion, lemon juice, Worcestershire sauce, horseradish, smoked paprika, cayenne pepper, salt, and pepper. Transfer to a 7-cup glass bowl.

3 Preheat oven to broiler at 500°F.

4 Add water to the Instant Pot® and insert steam rack. Place glass bowl on steam rack. Lock lid.

5 Press the Manual or Pressure Cook button and adjust cook time to 8 minutes. When timer beeps, quick-release pressure until float valve drops and then unlock lid. Sprinkle Parmesan cheese on top.

6 Place dip under broiler for 5 minutes to brown Parmesan. Serve warm.

Bangin' Party Shrimp

The only thing better than sharing some brew with a group of friends is cooking with the beer and sharing your appetizer with your friends! If you do not partake, just substitute the beer with water or broth. All options are yummy, as it is the addictive sauce that really brings this shrimp to life.

- **Hands-On Time: 5 minutes**
- **Cook Time: 0 minutes**

Serves 10

Dipping Sauce
½ cup mayonnaise
¼ cup sour cream
¼ cup Thai sweet chili sauce
1 tablespoon sriracha
2 teaspoons lime juice

Shrimp
1 (12-ounce) bottle gluten-
    free beer
4 pounds large uncooked
    shrimp, peeled and
    deveined

1 Combine dipping sauce ingredients in a small bowl. Refrigerate covered until ready to serve.

2 Pour beer into the Instant Pot® and insert steamer basket. Place shrimp in basket. Lock lid.

3 Press the Steam button and adjust cook time to 0 minutes. When timer beeps, quick-release pressure until float valve drops and then unlock lid.

4 Transfer shrimp to serving dish and serve warm or cold with dipping sauce.

Chinese Chicken Wings

The Instant Pot® lends a tenderness to the inside of the wings, and the oven gives a crispiness to the skin. In addition, the sweet, spicy, and umami flavors from the remaining ingredients take these wings over the top. The toasted sesame seed garnish provides the final texture element that sets each bite apart from all other recipes. And by making this quick and homemade sauce, you are avoiding those gluten fillers that are hidden in so many processed condiments.

- **Hands-On Time: 10 minutes**
- **Cook Time: 16 minutes**

Serves 6

¼ cup tamari

¼ cup apple cider vinegar

1 teaspoon sriracha

2 teaspoons Chinese five-spice powder

1 tablespoon light brown sugar

3 cloves garlic, peeled and minced

2 tablespoons sesame oil

5 scallions, sliced and separated into whites and greens

3 pounds chicken wings, separated at the joint

1 cup water

¼ cup toasted sesame seeds

WHAT'S IN CHINESE FIVE-SPICE POWDER?

This spice blend is a mixture typically consisting of cinnamon, cloves, star anise, peppercorns, and fennel seeds. Variations can include ginger, turmeric, nutmeg, and a number of other combinations depending on the brand, region, and even the dish being prepared.

1 In a large bowl, combine tamari, apple cider vinegar, sriracha, Chinese five-spice powder, brown sugar, garlic, sesame oil, and whites of scallions. Transfer 2 tablespoons of sauce to a small bowl and set aside.

2 Add wings to sauce in large bowl and toss. Refrigerate covered at least 1 hour or up to overnight.

3 Add water to the Instant Pot® and insert steamer basket. Place chicken wings in basket, arranging them so they aren't sitting on top of one another; place them standing up if necessary. Lock lid.

4 Press the Manual or Pressure Cook button and adjust cook time to 10 minutes. When timer beeps, let pressure release naturally for 5 minutes. Quick-release any additional pressure until float valve drops and then unlock lid.

5 Using a slotted spoon, transfer wings to a baking sheet. Brush with 2 tablespoons of reserved sauce. Broil wings 3 minutes on each side to crisp the chicken.

6 Transfer wings to a serving dish and garnish with sesame seeds and greens of scallions.

PB&J Wings

This classic combination of grape jelly and peanut butter is a natural complement to the humble chicken wing. And all three ingredients fit right in with the gluten-free way of living! Let your imagination go wild with all of the jelly flavors available. Try jalapeño jelly garnished with cilantro for a Mexican twist. Try fig jam garnished with goat cheese crumbles for your fancy-pants crowd. Imagination is the only limit when choosing new combinations.

- **Hands-On Time: 10 minutes**
- **Cook Time: 16 minutes**

Serves 6

½ cup smooth peanut butter
1 cup grape jelly
½ teaspoon sriracha
¼ cup white wine vinegar
3 pounds chicken wings, separated at the joint
1 cup water
¼ cup crushed peanuts

WHAT IS SRIRACHA?

Sriracha is the popular red hot sauce in the squeeze bottle with that recognizable rooster! The sauce is a mixture of fermented chili pepper paste, distilled vinegar, garlic, sugar, and salt. A little goes a long way, so add this addictive condiment slowly!

1. In a large bowl, combine peanut butter, jelly, sriracha, and white wine vinegar. Transfer 2 tablespoons of mixture to a small bowl and set aside.

2. Add wings to mixture in large bowl and toss. Refrigerate covered at least 1 hour or up to overnight.

3. Add water to the Instant Pot® and insert steamer basket. Place chicken wings in basket, arranging them so they aren't sitting on top of one another; place them standing up if necessary. Lock lid.

4. Press the Manual or Pressure Cook button and adjust cook time to 10 minutes. When timer beeps, let pressure release naturally for 5 minutes. Quick-release any additional pressure until float valve drops and then unlock lid.

5. Using a slotted spoon, transfer wings to a baking sheet. Brush with 2 tablespoons of reserved sauce. Broil wings 3 minutes on each side to crisp the chicken.

6. Transfer wings to a serving dish, garnish with crushed peanuts, and serve warm.

Crunchy Surprise Deviled Eggs

The dill pickle–flavored potato chips in this recipe are a fun flavor addition, and the crunchiness lends great texture. Salt and vinegar chips are also a good choice if you can't find the dill pickle variety. And let's just be honest—plain chips would be yummy too!

- **Hands-On Time: 15 minutes**
- **Cook Time: 4 minutes**

Yields 12 deviled eggs

1 cup water
6 large eggs
3 tablespoons mayonnaise
1 teaspoon yellow mustard
½ teaspoon dill pickle juice
1 teaspoon finely diced dill pickles
⅛ teaspoon smoked paprika
⅛ teaspoon salt
⅛ teaspoon ground black pepper
½ cup crushed dill pickle–flavored potato chips

THE DIFFERENCES BETWEEN SMOKED, SWEET, AND HOT PAPRIKA

All three spices are powders made from dried red peppers; however, each one comes from a pepper with a different kind of heat, as noted by their names: smoky, sweet, or hot. Smoked paprika, as long as it is not labeled as "hot," has a sweeter and smoky flavor.

1 Add water to the Instant Pot® and insert steamer basket. Place eggs in basket. Lock lid.

2 Press the Manual or Pressure Cook button and adjust cook time to 4 minutes. When timer beeps, quick-release pressure until float valve drops and then unlock lid.

3 Create an ice bath by adding a cup of ice and a cup of water to a medium bowl. Transfer eggs to ice bath to stop the cooking process.

4 Peel eggs. Slice each egg in half lengthwise and place yolks in a small bowl. Place egg white halves on a serving tray.

5 Add mayonnaise, mustard, pickle juice, diced pickles, smoked paprika, salt, and pepper to the small bowl with yolks. Use a fork to blend until smooth.

6 Spoon yolk filling into egg white halves. Sprinkle on crushed chips right before serving so they don't get soggy.

Refried Black Bean Dip

Loaded with flavor, this bean dip will disappear in no time around your guests. The Instant Pot® allows you to cook these beans without having to take time to soak them. If you want to cut prep time even more, substitute two cans of black beans and reduce the cooking time from 39 minutes to 7 minutes.

- **Hands-On Time: 5 minutes**
- **Cook Time: 39 minutes**

Serves 6

1 tablespoon olive oil

1 small red onion, peeled and diced

3 cloves garlic, peeled and minced

1 cup dried black beans, rinsed

1½ cups chicken broth

2 teaspoons chili powder

2 teaspoons ground cumin

1 teaspoon salt

¼ teaspoon cayenne pepper

1 (4-ounce) can diced green chiles, including juice

1 (14.5-ounce) can diced tomatoes, including juice

½ cup sour cream

1 Press the Sauté button on the Instant Pot®. Heat oil 30 seconds. Add onion to pot. Stir-fry 5 minutes until onions are translucent. Add garlic. Heat for an additional minute.

2 Add black beans, broth, chili powder, cumin, salt, cayenne pepper, green chiles with juice, and tomatoes with juice to pot and stir to combine. Lock lid.

3 Press the Beans button and cook for the default time of 30 minutes. When timer beeps, let pressure release naturally until float valve drops and then unlock lid.

4 Use an immersion blender to blend the dip in pot until smooth or use a stand blender to blend the dip in batches. With dip still in pot, press the Sauté button on the Instant Pot® and heat for 3 minutes, stirring several times.

5 Transfer dip to a serving dish. Garnish with sour cream and serve.

Roasted Red Pepper Hummus

This type of hummus can be found at most grocery stores, but you can now make a homemade and less expensive version of one of the most popular flavors. The addition of the roasted red peppers smooths out this creamy Middle Eastern dish staple.

- **Hands-On Time: 10 minutes**
- **Cook Time: 30 minutes**

Yields 1½ cups

½ cup dried chickpeas (also called garbanzo beans)

2 cups water

1 cup jarred roasted red peppers with liquid, chopped and divided

1 tablespoon tahini paste

2 cloves garlic, peeled and minced

1 tablespoon lemon juice

1 teaspoon lemon zest

¼ teaspoon ground cumin

¼ teaspoon smoked paprika

⅛ teaspoon cayenne pepper

¼ teaspoon salt

1 teaspoon sesame oil

1 tablespoon olive oil

1 Add chickpeas and water to the Instant Pot®. Drain liquid from jar of roasted peppers into pot. Set aside drained peppers. Lock lid. Press the Beans button and cook for the default time of 30 minutes. When timer beeps, let pressure release naturally for 5 minutes. Quick-release any additional pressure until float valve drops and then unlock lid.

2 Drain pot, reserving liquid in a small bowl.

3 Transfer chickpeas from pot into a food processor or stand blender. Add all but ¼ cup chopped red peppers, tahini paste, garlic, lemon juice, lemon zest, cumin, smoked paprika, cayenne pepper, salt, sesame oil, and olive oil. If consistency is too thick, slowly add reserved liquid, 1 table-spoon at a time. You are looking for a loose paste consistency.

4 Transfer hummus to a serving dish. Garnish with remaining chopped roasted red peppers and serve.

HOW DO YOU MAKE TAHINI?

Also known as *Ardeh*, tahini is a Middle Eastern paste made from ground toasted sesame seeds. To make your own quick tahini, pulse 1 cup of toasted sesame seeds in a food processor along with 3 tablespoons of olive oil, slowly pulsing in 1 tablespoon of oil at a time until a thin paste forms. Add ⅛ teaspoon of salt, if desired.

Taco Tuesday Hummus

This Mexican twist on a Middle Eastern dip just makes sense. The chickpeas replace the traditional black beans or pinto beans found in Mexican foods and, mixed with the appropriate spices, make an incredible new "bean dip." Serve with sliced gluten-free bread, corn chips, or crudités.

- **Hands-On Time: 10 minutes**
- **Cook Time: 30 minutes**

Yields 1½ cups

Garnish

1 Roma tomato, seeded and small-diced

1 tablespoon peeled and finely diced red onion

2 tablespoons chopped fresh cilantro

1 teaspoon lime juice

1 clove garlic, peeled and minced

⅛ teaspoon cayenne pepper

⅛ teaspoon salt

Hummus

½ cup dried chickpeas (also called garbanzo beans)

2 cups water

1 tablespoon tahini paste

2 cloves garlic, peeled and minced

1 tablespoon lime juice

1 teaspoon lime zest

¼ teaspoon ground cumin

¼ teaspoon chili powder

¼ teaspoon salt

2 tablespoons olive oil

1 In small bowl, combine garnish ingredients. Refrigerate covered until ready to use.

2 Add chickpeas and water to the Instant Pot®. Lock lid.

3 Press the Beans button and cook for the default time of 30 minutes. When timer beeps, let pressure release naturally for 5 minutes. Quick-release any additional pressure until float valve drops and then unlock lid.

4 Drain pot and reserve water.

5 Transfer chickpeas from pot into a food processor or stand blender. Add tahini paste, garlic, lime juice, lime zest, cumin, chili powder, salt, and olive oil. If consistency is too thick, slowly add reserved water, 1 tablespoon at a time. You are looking for a loose paste consistency.

6 Transfer hummus to a serving dish. Garnish with tomato mixture and serve.

Sausage-Horseradish Stuffed Mushrooms

The horseradish in this recipe adds just enough zip to the flavor of the already delicious and creamy insides of these meaty mushroom bites. If you can't find gluten-free bread crumbs, simply bake a piece of gluten-free bread in the oven at 300°F for 5 minutes on each side to dry it out. Then place the bread in your food processor and pulse to desired consistency.

- **Hands-On Time: 10 minutes**
- **Cook Time: 7 minutes**

Yields 10 mushrooms

1 tablespoon olive oil

¼ pound ground pork sausage

1 tablespoon peeled and finely diced yellow onion

1 tablespoon gluten-free bread crumbs

1 tablespoon prepared horseradish

2 tablespoons cream cheese, room temperature

1 teaspoon yellow mustard

¼ teaspoon garlic salt

1 cup water

8 ounces whole baby bella mushrooms (approximately 10), stemmed

2 tablespoons chopped fresh Italian flat-leaf parsley

1 Press the Sauté button on the Instant Pot® and heat oil 30 seconds. Add sausage and onion to pot. Stir-fry 5 minutes until sausage is no longer pink.

2 Transfer mixture to a small bowl and use paper towels to dab off excess oil and fat. Add bread crumbs, horseradish, cream cheese, yellow mustard, and garlic salt.

3 Pour water into the Instant Pot®. Stuff an equal amount of mixture into each mushroom cap and place in steamer basket. Insert steamer basket in pot and lock lid.

4 Press the Manual or Pressure Cook button and adjust cook time to 2 minutes. Adjust pressure to Low. When timer beeps, quick-release pressure until float valve drops and then unlock lid.

5 Transfer mushrooms to a serving dish. Garnish with chopped parsley. Serve warm.

USE THOSE MUSHROOM STEMS

Clean and dice stems and place in a lidded container and refrigerate. These stems, which are usually discarded, are ideal additions to breakfast scrambles, omelets, sauces, homemade broth, and even superhealthy green smoothies!

Mini Reuben Potato Skins

These potato skins are so tender when cooked in your Instant Pot®; finish them off in the oven to create crispy edges. The smaller red potatoes used here are ideal for bite-sized appetizers for your partygoers to enjoy. Because of the potato's petite size, guests can feel a little less guilty and more likely to indulge. And you can be happy knowing that you stayed gluten-free without compromising on flavor.

- **Hands-On Time: 15 minutes**
- **Cook Time: 22 minutes**

Serves 10

4 tablespoons olive oil

2 pounds red potatoes (approximately 10), scrubbed

1 cup chicken broth

2 tablespoons unsalted butter, melted

1 cup shredded Swiss cheese

10 ounces thick-sliced corned beef, chopped

¼ cup sauerkraut, drained

2 tablespoons Russian dressing, divided

2 teaspoons caraway seeds

WHAT DO I DO WITH THE SCOOPED-OUT POTATO?

Don't throw away the leftover cooked potatoes. There are so many ways to use them. You can either mash them for later or add them to any meatloaf recipe. Even better, make potato cakes: just add salt, pepper, an egg, and a little cheese to the potatoes, and quick-fry the patties on your stovetop to accompany almost any dish!

1 Use a fork to pierce each potato four times. Set aside.

2 Press the Sauté button on the Instant Pot®. Heat oil 30 seconds, then add potatoes to pot. Coat all sides of potatoes with oil and sauté 5 minutes until browned. Add broth. Lock lid.

3 Press the Manual or Pressure Cook button and adjust cook time to 7 minutes. When timer beeps, quick-release pressure until float valve drops and then unlock lid.

4 Using a slotted spoon, transfer potatoes to a plate. Let cool 5 minutes until you can handle them.

5 Preheat oven to 350°F.

6 Cut potatoes in half lengthwise. Scoop out approximately half of the potato, creating a boat. Place boats on a baking sheet lined with parchment paper. Lightly brush potatoes with melted butter. Bake 5 minutes.

7 In a small bowl, combine Swiss cheese, corned beef, sauerkraut, and 1 tablespoon Russian dressing.

8 Distribute corned beef mixture among potato halves. Bake skins for an additional 5 minutes.

9 Remove potatoes from oven and drizzle with remaining Russian dressing. Garnish with caraway seeds and serve.

Sweet Potato Fries with Sriracha Ranch Dipping Sauce

Tender on the inside and crispy on the outside, these will be your favorite sweet potato fries ever. You'll want to cook all root veggies like this, including white potatoes, turnips, and even rutabagas. Get creative with a variety of gluten-free dipping sauces and aioli for a new experience each time.

- **Hands-On Time: 10 minutes**
- **Cook Time: 13 minutes**

Serves 2

Sriracha Ranch Dipping Sauce
¼ cup mayonnaise
2 tablespoons sour cream
2 teaspoons sriracha
1 teaspoon chopped fresh dill
1 clove garlic, peeled and minced
½ teaspoon lemon juice
¼ teaspoon salt

Sweet Potato Fries
1 large sweet potato, peeled, trimmed, and cut into ½" sticks
2 tablespoons olive oil
1 teaspoon salt
½ teaspoon ground black pepper
½ teaspoon garlic powder
1 cup water

1 Line a baking sheet with parchment paper and set aside. Preheat oven to 425°F.

2 Combine Sriracha Ranch Dipping Sauce ingredients in a small bowl. Refrigerate covered until ready to use.

3 Place sweet potato sticks in a medium bowl and toss with oil, salt, pepper, and garlic powder.

4 Add water to the Instant Pot® and insert steamer basket. Add fries to basket. Lock lid.

5 Press the Steam button and adjust cook time to 3 minutes. When timer beeps, quick-release pressure until float valve drops and then unlock lid.

6 Transfer fries to the prepared baking sheet and scatter evenly. Bake 10 minutes until crisp and browned, tossing once halfway through cooking.

7 Transfer fries to serving dish. Serve warm with chilled dipping sauce.

Sriracha Lentil-Beef Sliders

When serving to a large group, cutting the beef with lentils or other legumes not only helps cut the cost drastically; it also adds an added layer and depth of flavor. Although the lentils can be cooked in water, using beef broth helps infuse some of that beefy flavor. Using beef with a makeup of 80/20 is optimal, because the natural fat lends the preferred juiciness, yielding a patty that isn't dried out.

- **Hands-On Time: 15 minutes**
- **Cook Time: 25 minutes**

Yields 15 sliders

1 cup dried yellow lentils

2 cups beef broth

½ pound 80/20 ground beef

½ cup finely chopped old-fashioned oats

2 large eggs

2 tablespoons peeled and finely diced yellow onion

2 teaspoons sriracha

½ teaspoon salt

1 Add lentils and broth to the Instant Pot®. Lock lid.

2 Press the Manual or Pressure Cook button and adjust the cook time to 15 minutes. When timer beeps, let pressure release naturally for 10 minutes. Quick-release any additional pressure until float valve drops and then unlock lid.

3 Drain liquid from pot and transfer lentils to a medium bowl. Using the back of a wooden spoon, smash most of the lentils, leaving the consistency somewhat chunky. Add beef, oats, eggs, onion, sriracha, and salt. Form mixture into fifteen slider patties.

4 Cook on stovetop over medium-high heat for 5 minutes per side.

5 Transfer patties to serving dish and serve warm.

Broccoli-Sausage Tater Tots

Everyone loves a good Tater Tot but not all that deep-frying. Add broccoli for nutrients and sausage for the yum factor, and this gluten-free Tater Tot hybrid will be a new family favorite! It is also fun for the little ones to help form the tots before baking.

- **Hands-On Time: 15 minutes**
- **Cook Time: 37 minutes**

Yields 20 tots

1 cup water

2 cups fresh broccoli florets

2 cups shredded russet potatoes, scrubbed

¼ pound breakfast pork sausage

1 shallot, peeled and finely minced

1 large egg

1 teaspoon dried oregano leaves

½ teaspoon salt

1 Add water to the Instant Pot® and insert steamer basket. Add broccoli and potatoes to basket. Lock lid.

2 Press the Manual or Pressure Cook button and adjust cook time to 2 minutes. When timer beeps, quick-release pressure until float valve drops and then unlock lid.

3 Preheat oven to 400°F. Line a baking sheet with parchment paper.

4 Transfer broccoli and potatoes to a food processor or blender. Pulse five times until smooth.

5 Transfer to a medium bowl. Add sausage, shallot, egg, oregano, and salt. Combine until well mixed.

6 Form mixture into twenty tots and place on the prepared baking sheet. Bake 35 minutes.

7 Transfer tots to serving dish and serve warm.

Green Enchilada Sauce

Green Enchilada Sauce, spiced and tart, can be a fresh homemade sauce to use on a dish of enchiladas made with gluten-free tortillas. It can also be used to cook with chicken in the Instant Pot®, served as a garnish with morning eggs, or even ladled over rice or gluten-free pasta.

- **Hands-On Time: 5 minutes**
- **Cook Time: 2 minutes**

Serves 8

1 pound tomatillos, halved, with outer husks discarded

Water

1 small yellow onion, peeled and diced

3 cloves garlic, peeled and minced

2 (4-ounce) cans diced green chiles

½ cup chopped fresh cilantro

1 teaspoon ground cumin

2 teaspoons salt

1½ cups chicken broth

1 Place tomatillos in the Instant Pot®. Add enough water to cover tomatillos. Lock lid.

2 Press the Manual or Pressure Cook button and adjust timer to 2 minutes. When timer beeps, let pressure release naturally until float valve drops and then unlock lid. Drain pot.

3 Add tomatillos, onion, garlic, green chiles, cilantro, cumin, salt, and broth to a food processor or blender. Pulse for 2 minutes until well combined.

4 Transfer sauce to a serving dish, cover, and chill in the refrigerator before using.

Meatless Spaghetti Sauce

Homemade anything is just better for us, in terms of both taste and unprocessed ingredients. Taking a little extra time with fresh vegetables such as celery, carrot, red onion, and garlic will add a freshness to your dish. Although many tomato sauces are gluten-free, research should be done on the brand, as cross contamination can sometimes be a problem.

- **Hands-On Time: 10 minutes**
- **Cook Time: 10 minutes**

Yields 4 cups

1 (28-ounce) can crushed tomatoes, including juice

1 stalk celery, finely diced

1 medium carrot, peeled and finely diced

½ medium red onion, peeled and finely diced

4 cloves garlic, peeled and quartered

2 tablespoons chopped fresh basil leaves

2 tablespoons chopped fresh Italian flat-leaf parsley

1 tablespoon fresh thyme leaves

1 teaspoon salt

½ teaspoon ground black pepper

½ cup beef broth

1 Combine all ingredients in the Instant Pot®. Lock lid.

2 Press the Manual or Pressure Cook button and adjust cook time to 10 minutes. When timer beeps, let pressure release naturally for 5 minutes. Quick-release any additional pressure until float valve drops and then unlock lid.

3 Use an immersion blender to blend the sauce in pot until desired consistency or use a stand blender to blend the sauce in batches.

4 Pour sauce into a lidded container or jar and refrigerate until ready to use. Use within five days.

Italian Ragù Sauce

Ragù and Bolognese sauces are similar in that they are both basic Italian meat sauces. Recipes will differ depending on the region or family from which the sauce originates. But one consistent difference is that ragù contains red wine, and Bolognese contains white wine. So, whichever wine you have on hand, go for it. The Instant Pot® will have you thinking that this sauce has been simmering on Nonna's stove for hours.

- **Hands-On Time: 10 minutes**
- **Cook Time: 21 minutes**

Yields 3 cups

1 tablespoon olive oil

1 small yellow onion, peeled and diced

1 medium carrot, scrubbed and diced

1 stalk celery, diced

2 slices bacon, diced

½ pound ground pork

½ pound ground beef

4 cloves garlic, peeled and minced

4 ounces dry red wine

1 (15-ounce) can tomato sauce

½ cup beef broth

1 teaspoon salt

½ teaspoon ground black pepper

¼ cup whole milk

1. Press the Sauté button on the Instant Pot®. Heat oil 30 seconds. Add onion, carrot, and celery to pot. Stir-fry 3 minutes until onions are tender. Add bacon, pork, and beef, and heat 5 minutes until meat is no longer pink. Add garlic and heat for an additional minute. Add red wine and stir for 2 minutes, allowing alcohol to burn off.

2. Add tomato sauce, beef broth, salt, and pepper to pot and stir to combine. Lock lid.

3. Press the Manual or Pressure Cook button and adjust cook time to 10 minutes. When timer beeps, let pressure release naturally until float valve drops and then unlock lid. Stir in milk.

4. Use immediately or store lidded in refrigerator and use within 3 days or in the freezer for up to 4 months.

RAGÙ OR RAGOUT?

Although pronounced the same way, ragù and ragout are two completely different things. Ragù is a simple Italian meat sauce, as the preceding recipe indicates. Ragout is a French sauce that has a stew-like consistency, more liquid, and often contains vegetables as well as beef, poultry, or seafood.

5

Side Dishes

With our busy lives, it is a shame that when cooking meals we often skip the nutritious veggies and tasty sides that we should be eating. All the while, those well-intentioned vegetables take a back seat in the refrigerator until they spoil. Not only is it a waste of healthful food; it is also a big waste of money. And on a gluten-free diet, our bodies are sometimes depleted of that healthy fiber traditionally obtained from breads and other gluten-filled foods. So, fiber-filled veggies are a crucial part of the equation to compensate for a possible fiber deficiency. And veggies don't have to be boring. They are fresh, tasty, and filled with nutrients.

With the Instant Pot®, you can have flavorful seasonal vegetables in minutes while the main dish is being prepared. Also, vegetables cooked in your Instant Pot® retain more nutrients than if they were boiled on the stovetop or roasted in the oven. So, while you're grilling that steak outdoors in the summer or charring some chicken on an indoor grilling pan, why not take just a few minutes to round out the meal? With recipes such as Hearty Garlic Mushrooms, Green Beans with Slivered Almonds, Citrus Quinoa, and Cooked Green Cabbage, you will be happy you took the extra time to prepare a side dish. And your body will thank you too!

Creamy Bacon-Corn Casserole

This is just one of those creamy, bacon-y sides that should only be made for special occasions; otherwise you'd devour it each night, and your waistline would not approve! Easy yet decadent and surprisingly gluten-free, this complete comfort dish will hit all of those happy taste buds.

- **Hands-On Time: 5 minutes**
- **Cook Time: 17 minutes**

Serves 4

6 slices bacon, quartered

1 small red bell pepper, seeded and diced

¼ cup whole milk

2 tablespoons gluten-free all-purpose flour

2 tablespoons unsalted butter, melted

2 ounces cream cheese, room temperature

½ teaspoon salt

½ teaspoon ground black pepper

2 (15.25-ounce) cans corn, drained

2 tablespoons Parmesan cheese

1 cup water

1 Press the Sauté button on the Instant Pot®. Add bacon to pot and cook 5 minutes until crisp. Transfer bacon to a paper towel–lined plate. Crumble when cooled.

2 Add bell pepper to pot and cook 5 minutes in bacon drippings until tender.

3 In medium bowl, whisk together milk and flour. Add butter, cream cheese, salt, and pepper. Add crumbled bacon, bell pepper, and corn.

4 Transfer to a 7-cup glass dish. Sprinkle with Parmesan cheese.

5 Add water to the Instant Pot®. Lock lid.

6 Press the Manual or Pressure Cook button and adjust cook time to 7 minutes. When timer beeps, let pressure release naturally for 5 minutes. Quick-release any additional pressure until float valve drops and then unlock lid.

7 Remove dish from the Instant Pot® and let cool for 10 minutes. Serve warm.

Brussels Sprouts Hash

Let's face it, sometimes the slightly bitter Brussels sprout needs a little love to make it palatable to some. That's where the smokiness of the bacon, the sweetness of the syrup and potato, and the bright citrus from the orange come into play. These flavors cut the bitterness from the sprouts and are a great addition to your gluten-free plate. I dare you to not love this side dish!

- **Hands-On Time: 5 minutes**
- **Cook Time: 10 minutes**

Serves 4

4 slices bacon, quartered

1 medium red onion, peeled and sliced

1 medium sweet potato, peeled and small-diced

1 pound Brussels sprouts, trimmed and halved

1 cup water

2 tablespoons maple syrup

2 tablespoons fresh orange juice

⅛ teaspoon hot sauce

1 tablespoon chopped fresh chives

1 Press the Sauté button on the Instant Pot®. Add bacon to pot and stir-fry 5 minutes until bacon is crisp and the fat is rendered. Transfer bacon to a paper towel–lined plate and crumble when cooled.

2 Add onion, sweet potato, and Brussels sprouts to the Instant Pot® and stir-fry for an additional 2 minutes in bacon drippings. Remove veggies from pot.

3 Add water to pot and insert steamer basket. Add veggies to basket. Lock lid.

4 Press the Manual or Pressure Cook button and adjust cook time to 3 minutes. When timer beeps, quick-release pressure until float valve drops and then unlock lid.

5 Transfer cooked veggies to a serving dish. Toss with maple syrup, orange juice, and hot sauce. Garnish with crumbled bacon and chives. Serve warm.

Hearty Garlic Mushrooms

Mushrooms are hearty on their own, but cooking them in beef broth adds another layer of meatiness to their rustic nature. Add butter and garlic, and, well, need anything else be said? Serve this with a steak and mashed potatoes with a little gravy, and you'll never want another meal again. Life will be complete!

- **Hands-On Time: 5 minutes**
- **Cook Time: 15 minutes**

Serves 4

3 tablespoons unsalted butter

4 cloves garlic, peeled and minced

1 pound whole button mushrooms, cleaned

2 cups beef broth

2 teaspoons Worcestershire sauce

1 tablespoon fresh thyme leaves

⅛ teaspoon salt

1 Press the Sauté button on the Instant Pot®. Heat butter 30 seconds. Add garlic to pot and cook for 1 minute. Add mushrooms and stir-fry for an additional minute. Add broth and Worcestershire sauce. Lock lid.

2 Press the Manual or Pressure Cook button and adjust cook time to 13 minutes. When timer beeps, let pressure release naturally for 5 minutes. Quick-release any additional pressure until float valve drops and then unlock lid.

3 Using a slotted spoon, transfer mushrooms to a serving dish. Garnish with fresh thyme leaves and salt, and serve.

Simple "Baked" Potatoes

Instead of baking potatoes in the oven, you can cut your cooking time drastically with the Instant Pot®. It's a perfect alternative to warming up your house with a hot oven in the summer. Serve with butter, sour cream, chives, grated Cheddar cheese, or leftover chili!

- **Hands-On Time: 5 minutes**
- **Cook Time: 10 minutes**

Serves 4

1 cup water

4 medium russet potatoes, scrubbed

1 Add water to the Instant Pot® and insert steamer basket. Add potatoes to basket. Lock lid.

2 Press the Manual or Pressure Cook button and adjust cook time to 10 minutes. When timer beeps, let pressure release naturally until float valve drops and then unlock lid.

3 Transfer potatoes to serving dish and serve warm.

Garlic Parmesan Fingerling Potatoes

Fingerling potatoes are small but mighty in their sweet flavor and tenderness. Their stubby size can work with the schedule of the busy home chef. There is no need to peel or dice these small tubers: just give them a good scrub, and they are ready for steamed perfection in the Instant Pot®.

- **Hands-On Time: 5 minutes**
- **Cook Time: 11 minutes**

Serves 6

2 tablespoons unsalted butter, divided

1½ pounds fingerling potatoes, scrubbed

4 cloves garlic, peeled and chopped

2 cups water

1 teaspoon salt

½ teaspoon ground black pepper

2 tablespoons sour cream

½ cup grated Parmesan cheese

2 tablespoons chopped fresh chives

1. Use a fork to pierce each potato three times.

2. Press the Sauté button on the Instant Pot®. Heat 1 tablespoon butter 30 seconds, then add potatoes to pot. Stir-fry 4 minutes. Add garlic and heat for an additional minute.

3. Add water to the Instant Pot®. Lock lid.

4. Press the Manual or Pressure Cook button and adjust cook time to 6 minutes. When timer beeps, quick-release pressure until float valve drops and then unlock lid.

5. Using a slotted spoon, transfer potatoes to a serving dish. Toss with remaining butter, salt, pepper, sour cream, and Parmesan cheese. Garnish with chopped chives. Serve warm.

Cauliflower with Cheddar Sauce

Cheese makes everyone happy, especially those picky eaters in your life. So, next time you are in the produce section, pick up that inexpensive and fresh head of cauliflower rich in vitamins and minerals. This simple recipe will have your family licking their plates.

- **Hands-On Time: 5 minutes**
- **Cook Time: 7 minutes**

Serves 4

1 cup water

1 large head cauliflower, cut into florets

1 tablespoon unsalted butter

½ cup grated Cheddar cheese

¾ cup whole milk

1 tablespoon gluten-free all-purpose flour

½ teaspoon salt

½ teaspoon ground black pepper

1 Add water to the Instant Pot® and insert steamer basket. Add cauliflower to basket. Lock lid.

2 Press the Steam button and adjust cook time to 5 minutes. When timer beeps, quick-release pressure until float valve drops and then unlock lid.

3 Transfer cauliflower to a serving dish and drain pot.

4 Press the Sauté button on the Instant Pot® and heat butter 30 seconds. Add cheese, milk, flour, salt, and pepper. Whisk for 2 minutes until smooth.

5 Pour sauce over cauliflower in dish and serve warm.

WHAT OTHER CHEESE VARIETIES WORK WITH CAULIFLOWER?

Although this is a matter of taste, many different cheeses and cheese combinations can go with the very mild yet mighty cauliflower. You can cut in some cream cheese or mascarpone with the Cheddar, make a creamy Mornay sauce, or even use the sweet and salty Gouda, which melts into a rich sea of yum! Herbs can be added to any of these sauces to change things up even more.

Smashed Garlic-Parm Purple Potatoes

When you don't feel like breaking out the mixer or ricer, you can use the back of a fork. This quick method is especially great for those who like lumpy mashed potatoes. Baby reds or yellow potatoes can be used as a substitute for the purple potatoes, or you can even use a mixture of all three.

- **Hands-On Time: 10 minutes**
- **Cook Time: 10 minutes**

Serves 6

4 tablespoons unsalted butter, divided

1½ pounds baby purple potatoes, scrubbed

3 cloves garlic, peeled and minced

2 cups water

2 tablespoons Parmesan cheese

¼ cup whole milk

1 teaspoon salt

½ teaspoon ground black pepper

1 Use a fork to pierce each potato four times. Press the Sauté button on the Instant Pot®. Heat 2 tablespoons butter 30 seconds and add potatoes and garlic to pot. Sauté 3 minutes, stirring frequently.

2 Add water to the Instant Pot®. Lock lid.

3 Press the Manual or Pressure Cook button and adjust cook time to 7 minutes. When timer beeps, quick-release pressure until float valve drops and then unlock lid.

4 Using a slotted spoon, transfer the potatoes to a serving bowl. Toss with remaining butter, Parmesan, milk, salt, and pepper.

5 Using an immersion blender or the back of a fork, gently mash potatoes until desired consistency. Serve warm.

CAN I LEAVE THE SKIN ON POTATOES?

If taking the time to peel your potatoes drives you crazy, just stop. Those skins are full of fiber, iron, and vitamins C and B$_6$. But make sure you buy organic potatoes; otherwise you may be ingesting some of the chemicals used in cultivating a crop.

Quinoa Tabbouleh

Though traditionally made with bulgur, which is cracked wheat, this tabbouleh gets a protein-packed punch along with the tasty flavor of quinoa as a substitute. Ideal as a side dish around the family table or as a tasty treat for a picnic, this dish can be whipped up in no time—and no one will be the wiser of your substitution.

- **Hands-On Time: 10 minutes**
- **Cook Time: 20 minutes**

Serves 4

1 cup quinoa
1¾ cups water
1 tablespoon olive oil
3 tablespoons lemon juice
½ teaspoon salt
1 English cucumber, peeled and diced
2 Roma tomatoes, seeded and diced
1 tablespoon lemon zest
2 scallions, thinly sliced
½ teaspoon ground black pepper
⅓ cup chopped fresh parsley
⅓ cup chopped fresh mint leaves

1   Add quinoa, water, olive oil, lemon juice, and salt to the Instant Pot®. Stir well. Lock lid.

2   Press the Porridge button and cook for the default time of 20 minutes. When timer beeps, quick-release pressure until float valve drops and then unlock lid.

3   Transfer quinoa to a serving dish and fluff with a fork. Toss in cucumber, tomatoes, lemon zest, scallions, black pepper, parsley, and mint.

4   Refrigerate covered at least 1 hour or up to overnight. Serve chilled.

WHAT IS AN ENGLISH CUCUMBER?
The English cucumber is longer and more slender than the traditional cucumber. You will generally find it wrapped in plastic. Although it is considered "seedless," its seeds are just smaller and softer, making them easier to eat. If you cannot find an English cucumber, you can use a traditional cucumber instead.

Citrus Quinoa

While you are tending to the grill with some juicy chicken breasts and colorful bell peppers, let your Instant Pot® make this side dish of bright Citrus Quinoa to complete the meal. Quinoa, pronounced "keen-wah," is a flowering plant in the amaranth family and is rich in magnesium. Some folks who have gluten intolerances are also lactose intolerant, which deprives them of magnesium often found in dairy products. Quinoa helps aid in this deficiency.

- **Hands-On Time: 5 minutes**
- **Cook Time: 20 minutes**

Serves 4

1 cup quinoa
1¾ cups water
2 tablespoons unsalted butter
2 tablespoons lemon juice
2 tablespoons lime juice
½ teaspoon salt

1 Add quinoa, water, butter, lemon juice, lime juice, and salt to the Instant Pot®. Stir well. Lock lid.

2 Press the Porridge button and cook for the default time of 20 minutes. When timer beeps, quick-release pressure until float valve drops and then unlock lid.

3 Transfer quinoa to a serving dish and fluff with a fork. Serve warm.

Buttery Cooked Carrots

Carrots are a great, inexpensive way to bump up the nutrition on your plate. This simply seasoned side dish can accompany almost any main dish. Cut the carrots in equal sizes so that this humble root veggie cooks evenly. To increase the flavor, try garlic salt instead of regular salt. Also, you can garnish the carrots with chopped parsley or fresh thyme leaves.

- **Hands-On Time: 5 minutes**
- **Cook Time: 5 minutes**

Serves 6

1 pound carrots, scrubbed, peeled, and large-diced
1 cup water
2 tablespoons unsalted butter
½ teaspoon salt

1 Add carrots and water to the Instant Pot®. Lock lid.

2 Press the Manual or Pressure Cook button and adjust cook time to 5 minutes. When timer beeps, quick-release pressure until float valve drops and then unlock lid.

3 Using a slotted spoon, transfer the carrots to a serving dish. Toss with butter and salt. Serve warm.

Red Cabbage and Apples

Known as *Rotkohl* in German, this popular side dish is modified by every *Oma* with her own secret recipe. And now you have your version! Serve this cabbage with a hearty roast, schnitzel made with gluten-free bread crumbs, bratwurst, or even a rotisserie chicken for a change of pace.

- **Hands-On Time: 10 minutes**
- **Cook Time: 4 minutes**

Serves 4

1 large head of red cabbage (approximately 2 pounds), cored and sliced into thin strips

2 large Granny Smith apples, peeled, cored, and diced

1 small sweet yellow onion, peeled and diced

½ teaspoon ground allspice

2 tablespoons light brown sugar

1 cup water

¼ cup apple cider vinegar

2 tablespoons unsalted butter

½ teaspoon salt

1 Add cabbage, apple, onion, allspice, brown sugar, water, and apple cider vinegar to the Instant Pot®. Lock lid.

2 Press the Manual or Pressure Cook button and adjust cook time to 4 minutes. When timer beeps, quick-release pressure until float valve drops and then unlock lid.

3 Using a slotted spoon, transfer the cabbage and apple mixture to a serving dish. Toss with butter and salt. Serve warm.

Steamed Yellow Summer Squash

Whether your garden is overflowing with yellow squash or zucchini, or you can't resist the beauties at your local roadside farmer stand, this recipe can help with your problem while providing you a perfect side dish for any protein-packed entrée—in minutes!

- **Hands-On Time: 10 minutes**
- **Cook Time: 6 minutes**

Serves 6

2 tablespoons unsalted butter

1 small sweet yellow onion, peeled and diced

4 medium yellow summer squash, sliced into ½" circles

1 teaspoon salt

1 teaspoon ground black pepper

1 Press the Sauté button on the Instant Pot®. Heat butter 30 seconds. Add onion to pot and stir-fry for 5 minutes until onions are translucent. Add remaining ingredients. Lock lid.

2 Press the Manual or Pressure Cook button and adjust cook time to 1 minute. When timer beeps, quick-release pressure until float valve drops and then unlock lid.

3 Transfer squash and onions to a serving dish. Serve warm.

Corn on the Cob

If you have never cooked corn on the cob in milk, then you are missing out. It mimics the natural milkiness of corn and makes it even more tender. The added salt and butter are the best accents to let the corn goodness shine. Also, don't get scared off if you hear the term *corn gluten*: it is not the same as the "bad" type of gluten that you are trying to avoid.

- **Hands-On Time: 5 minutes**
- **Cook Time: 2 minutes**

Yields 8 half ears of corn

1 cup whole milk

½ cup water

4 fresh ears of corn, shucked and halved

1 teaspoon salt

3 tablespoons unsalted butter, cut into several pats

1 Add milk, water, and corn to the Instant Pot®. Sprinkle with salt and place butter pats on the corn. Lock lid.

2 Press the Manual or Pressure Cook button and adjust cook time to 2 minutes. When timer beeps, quick-release pressure until float valve drops and then unlock lid. Toss corn twice in pot liquids.

3 Transfer corn to a serving dish and serve warm.

Southern-Style Collard Greens

Traditionally cooked for hours, collard greens can be cooked to perfection in just minutes in the Instant Pot®. You will taste the soul in this superfood side dish and take advantage of the long list of nutrients found in these inexpensive leafy greens. The ham hock (you can also use bacon, a ham bone, or diced ham) lends a smokiness, and the vinegar actually helps cut that bitterness that some people dislike when eating collards on their own.

- **Hands-On Time: 10 minutes**
- **Cook Time: 10 minutes**

Serves 6

2 **bunches collard greens, chopped (spines removed)**
1 **small sweet yellow onion, peeled and diced**
¼ **cup apple cider vinegar**
1 **teaspoon sriracha**
1 **smoked ham hock**
1 **cup chicken broth**
½ **teaspoon granulated sugar**
½ **teaspoon salt**
¼ **teaspoon ground black pepper**

1 Place all ingredients in the Instant Pot®. Lock lid.

2 Press the Manual or Pressure Cook button and adjust cook time to 10 minutes. When timer beeps, let pressure release naturally until float valve drops and then unlock lid. Flake off ham from bone into greens and discard bone.

3 Transfer to a serving dish and serve warm.

Blue Cheese Asparagus

What better complement to a grilled filet mignon than this Blue Cheese Asparagus! Look for bright green stalks with firm buds—so simple yet elegant. Coupled with a sexy date, a glass of Cabernet, and some sultry music, this is a meal meant for love.

- **Hands-On Time: 5 minutes**
- **Cook Time: 1 minute**

Serves 4

1 cup water

1 pound asparagus spears, woody ends trimmed and discarded

2 teaspoons olive oil

1 tablespoon balsamic vinegar

2 tablespoons crumbled blue cheese

2 tablespoons crushed walnuts

1 Add water to the Instant Pot®. Place asparagus evenly in steamer basket and place basket in pot. Lock lid.

2 Press the Manual or Pressure Cook button and adjust cook time to 1 minute. Quick-release pressure until float valve drops and then unlock lid.

3 Transfer asparagus to a serving dish and toss with oil and vinegar. Garnish with blue cheese and walnuts. Serve warm.

Orange Juice Beets

Beets are a superpower, containing nitrates that help dilate your blood vessels, leading to more stabilized blood pressure. They are also fantastic if you are looking for a natural food coloring, but because of this, peeling them can leave your fingers bright pink. There are many ways to rid yourself of beet stains: try lemon juice or simple baking soda, or even scrubbing your hands with a halved potato that has been dipped in coarse salt. And, there are always plastic gloves!

- **Hands-On Time: 10 minutes**
- **Cook Time: 10 minutes**

Serves 6

1 cup water
6 medium beets, ends trimmed
Juice of 1 medium orange
2 teaspoons unsalted butter
1 teaspoon salt

1 Add water to the Instant Pot® and insert steamer basket. Add beets to basket. Lock lid.

2 Press the Manual or Pressure Cook button and adjust cook time to 10 minutes. When timer beeps, quick-release pressure until float valve drops and then unlock lid.

3 Let beets rest 5 minutes. Once cool, peel off their outer skin with your hands. Cut beets into quarters and transfer to a serving dish.

4 Add orange juice, butter, and salt to dish. Toss and serve warm.

Green Beans with Slivered Almonds

Do you ever look at those gorgeous green beans at the farmers' market and don't know quite how to use them? The Instant Pot® steams them to perfection, while chicken broth lends the flavor that kicks this simple dish up a notch. The slivered almonds, containing fiber and healthy fats, lend a crunchy texture.

- **Hands-On Time: 10 minutes**
- **Cook Time: 3 minutes**

Serves 4

1 pound fresh green beans, rinsed and ends trimmed
2 cups chicken broth
1 teaspoon salt
2 tablespoons unsalted butter
¼ cup slivered almonds

1 Add beans and broth to the Instant Pot®. Lock lid.

2 Press the Manual or Pressure Cook button and adjust cook time to 3 minutes. When timer beeps, quick-release pressure until float valve drops and then unlock lid.

3 Add salt, butter, and almonds to pot and toss beans.

4 Transfer beans to a serving dish and serve warm.

Ranch Steamed Broccoli

Why don't some people like broccoli? Well, it might not be fair to label them as "picky eaters": due to human genetics, about 70 percent of people can detect a certain bitterness in broccoli. By adding a little lemon juice and a tasty, familiar seasoning like ranch, everyone can enjoy the benefits of this healthy little vegetable instead of hating every bite.

- **Hands-On Time: 5 minutes**
- **Cook Time: 0 minutes**

Serves 4

1 cup water
3½ cups chopped broccoli (approximately 1 medium head)
2 tablespoons unsalted butter
1 teaspoon lemon juice
2 tablespoons dry ranch seasoning
½ teaspoon salt

1 Add water to the Instant Pot®. Insert steamer basket and arrange broccoli in an even layer. Lock lid.

2 Press the Steam button and adjust cook time to 0 minutes. When timer beeps, quick-release pressure until float valve drops and then unlock lid.

3 Transfer broccoli to a serving dish and toss with remaining ingredients. Serve warm.

Basic Polenta

Polenta is a great side dish as well as a base for many meals, such as morning grits, shrimp and grits, and polenta croutons. To change up the flavor, add cheese to the polenta after cooking, replace the water with your favorite broth, or just add a handful of fresh herbs. This inexpensive and delicious corn derivative will be your new favorite starch!

- **Hands-On Time: 5 minutes**
- **Cook Time: 10 minutes**

Serves 6

5 cups water
1 cup polenta
2 tablespoons unsalted butter
1 teaspoon salt

1 Stir all ingredients together in the Instant Pot®. Lock lid.

2 Press the Manual or Pressure Cook button and adjust cook time to 10 minutes. When timer beeps, quick-release pressure until float valve drops and then unlock lid. Whisk polenta in pot 5 minutes until it thickens.

3 Transfer polenta to a serving dish and serve warm.

Cooked Green Cabbage

This cruciferous veggie is full of vitamin C and adds bulk to a meal without adding bulk to your waistline. Although this is an ideal low-calorie side to any meat dish, you can add slices of precooked smoked sausage before steaming for a tasty one-pot wonder!

- **Hands-On Time: 5 minutes**
- **Cook Time: 6 minutes**

Serves 4

2 tablespoons unsalted butter

2 slices bacon, diced

1 cup chicken broth

1 head green cabbage, chopped, hard midsection removed

1 teaspoon apple cider vinegar

½ teaspoon salt

1 Press the Sauté button on the Instant Pot®. Heat butter 30 seconds and add bacon to pot. Sauté 3 minutes, stirring frequently to render fat from bacon.

2 Add broth to pot, scraping any bits from the bottom and sides of pot. Add cabbage, vinegar, and salt. Lock lid.

3 Press the Manual or Pressure Cook button and adjust cook time to 3 minutes. When timer beeps, quick-release pressure until float valve drops and then unlock lid.

4 Using a slotted spoon, transfer cabbage to a serving dish. Serve warm.

6

Beans, Rice, and Gluten-Free Pasta

The pressure and steam of the Instant Pot® create deliciously moist and tender bean dishes, rice, and pasta. From Bacon Maple Baked Beans to Curried Chickpeas with Spinach, and from Egg Noodles with Creamy Mushroom Sauce to Minty Pea Risotto, you'll be whipping up some new and tasty dishes with ease. Beans are one of the foods that the Instant Pot® was made for. No more soaking those hard, little pebbles: put them straight in the pot, and they will be tender in under an hour. Plus, buying beans in bulk is much more economical.

And don't forget about the rice and pasta that can be cooked to perfection in the Instant Pot®. The gluten-free choices for pasta are endless, such as traditional gluten-free pasta made from corn or rice, chickpeas, lentils, or ancient grains. They all have a different taste and texture, so don't give up if the first one you try isn't satisfying. Have a gluten-free pasta taste test for a day of family fun and see which ones work for you!

Black-Eyed Peas Summer Salad

Served as a side dish or portioned into prep bowls for later meals, this salad is undeniably delicious. So, show up to a family event with this tasty side, and no one will know that it doesn't contain gluten. This dish is perfect for vegan, gluten-free, and omnivore friends alike, and everyone will want a second helping of this flavorful—and healthy—salad.

- **Hands-On Time: 15 minutes**
- **Cook Time: 30 minutes**

Serves 8

2 cups dried black-eyed peas, rinsed

4 cups chicken broth

1 teaspoon salt

¼ teaspoon ground black pepper

1 cucumber, peeled, seeded, and diced

2 Roma tomatoes, seeded and diced

½ medium red onion, peeled and diced

1 cup corn kernels

¼ cup crumbled feta cheese

2 tablespoons chopped fresh dill

2 teaspoons olive oil

1 Add peas and broth to the Instant Pot®. Lock lid.

2 Press the Beans button and cook for the default time of 30 minutes. When timer beeps, let pressure release naturally for 10 minutes. Quick-release any additional pressure until float valve drops and then unlock lid. Drain any extra liquid.

3 Transfer black-eyed peas to a medium bowl. Allow to cool 10 minutes.

4 Toss in remaining ingredients. Cover and refrigerate 30 minutes or up to overnight. Serve chilled.

Bacon Maple Baked Beans

The rich maple flavor gives these beans an edge. Show up to the picnic with these sweet and smoky baked beans and watch the smiles grow...there's no need to tell anyone that they are gluten-free! Great as a side or to put on burgers and hot dogs, this American side dish is a staple for all outdoor festivities.

- **Hands-On Time: 10 minutes**
- **Cook Time: 46 minutes**

1 tablespoon olive oil

5 slices bacon, diced

1 large sweet onion, peeled and diced

4 cloves garlic, peeled and minced

2 cups dried navy beans

4 cups chicken broth

2 teaspoons ground mustard

1 teaspoon salt

¼ teaspoon ground black pepper

½ cup pure maple syrup

½ cup ketchup

1 teaspoon smoked paprika

1 teaspoon Worcestershire sauce

1 teaspoon apple cider vinegar

1 Press the Sauté button on the Instant Pot®. Heat oil 30 seconds. Add bacon and onion to pot. Stir-fry for 5 minutes until onions are translucent. Add garlic and cook for an additional minute. Add beans. Toss to combine.

2 Add broth, mustard, salt, and pepper to the Instant Pot®. Lock lid.

3 Press the Beans button and cook for the default time of 30 minutes. When timer beeps, let pressure release naturally for 10 minutes. Quick-release any additional pressure until float valve drops and then unlock lid.

4 Stir in maple syrup, ketchup, smoked paprika, Worcestershire sauce, and vinegar. Press the Sauté button on the Instant Pot®, then press the Adjust button to change the heat to Less. Simmer uncovered for 10 minutes to thicken the sauce.

5 Transfer beans to a serving dish and serve warm.

Smoky Lima Beans

There is no soaking required when cooking dried beans in the Instant Pot®. Just give them a good rinse and throw out any undesirables. The bacon adds just the right amount of smokiness to this simple, inexpensive bean. A ham hock or ham bone can be subbed in for the bacon.

- **Hands-On Time: 5 minutes**
- **Cook Time: 30 minutes**

Serves 6

1 cup dried large lima beans, rinsed and picked over for undesirables
2 slices bacon, diced
1 teaspoon salt
4 cups water

1 Add lima beans, bacon, salt, and water to the Instant Pot®. Lock lid.

2 Press the Beans button and cook for the default time of 30 minutes. When timer beeps, let pressure release naturally for 10 minutes. Quick-release any additional pressure until float valve drops and then unlock lid. Drain any extra liquid.

3 Transfer lima beans to a serving dish and serve warm.

Coconut Lime Jasmine Rice

This side dish is a great complement to fish tacos and lends a smooth and cooling effect to a spicy curry dish. It is a simple side that is easy to make and fun to play around with, using different citrus fruits such as lemons, oranges, and even grapefruit. The addition of coconut milk is not only gluten-free; it also helps reduce cholesterol intake when swapped out for whole milk.

- **Hands-On Time: 5 minutes**
- **Cook Time: 3 minutes**

Serves 4

1 cup jasmine rice
¾ cup water
½ cup canned coconut milk
2 tablespoons lime juice
1 tablespoon lime zest
½ teaspoon salt
1 tablespoon unsalted butter

1 Place all ingredients into the Instant Pot®. Lock lid.

2 Press the Manual or Pressure Cook button and adjust cook time to 3 minutes. When timer beeps, let pressure release naturally for 5 minutes. Quick-release any additional pressure until float valve drops and then unlock lid.

3 Ladle rice into four bowls and serve warm.

Curried Chickpeas with Spinach

In addition to the curry powder and the nutmeg, the spices from this dish are remarkably fragrant and delicious. The chickpeas are supersatisfying to the tummy, and the spinach is packed with nutrients. Enjoy this recipe as a complete meal on Meatless Monday with a little Greek yogurt and a side of gluten-free naan or pita bread.

- **Hands-On Time: 5 minutes**
- **Cook Time: 34 minutes**

Serves 6

1 cup dried chickpeas (also called garbanzo beans), rinsed

4 cups water

1 (20-ounce) can tomato sauce

1 teaspoon garlic powder

¼ teaspoon ground ginger

1 tablespoon curry powder

⅛ teaspoon ground nutmeg

½ teaspoon salt

¼ teaspoon ground black pepper

2 cups fresh baby spinach

1 Add chickpeas and water to the Instant Pot®. Lock lid.

2 Press the Beans button and cook for the default time of 30 minutes. When timer beeps, let pressure release naturally for 10 minutes. Quick-release any additional pressure until float valve drops and then unlock lid. Drain any extra liquid.

3 Stir in remaining ingredients. Switch to low pressure and simmer 4 minutes to heat through and wilt spinach.

4 Transfer mixture to a serving dish and serve warm.

Tuscan Cannellini Beans

Tuscan food is described as very simple with no heavy sauces. As a matter of fact, olive oil is primarily used instead of butter, even with bread. If you cannot find cannellini beans, great northerns can be subbed although they are a slightly smaller bean and have a bit more of a tougher flesh than cannellini beans.

- **Hands-On Time: 5 minutes**
- **Cook Time: 30 minutes**

Serves 6

1 cup dried cannellini or white kidney beans, rinsed

1 (14.5-ounce) can diced tomatoes, including juice

1 small yellow onion, peeled and diced

1 teaspoon salt

2 cups water

¼ cup chopped fresh parsley

1 tablespoon olive oil

¼ cup shaved Parmesan cheese

1 Add beans, tomatoes with juice, onion, salt, and water to the Instant Pot®. Lock lid.

2 Press the Beans button and cook for the default time of 30 minutes. When timer beeps, let pressure release naturally for 10 minutes. Quick-release any additional pressure until float valve drops and then unlock lid. Drain any extra liquid.

3 Transfer bean mixture to a serving dish. Toss in parsley and olive oil. Garnish with Parmesan cheese and serve warm.

Egg Noodles with Creamy Mushroom Sauce

This is the perfect comfort dish to serve alongside a whole chicken. If you have leftover chicken, chop it up and add it to the noodle mixture for a complete meal. When heating up leftover noodles, add a little milk to the dish before warming to add more creaminess. And don't forget to make that superhealthy broth with the leftover bones.

- **Hands-On Time: 2 minutes**
- **Cook Time: 10 minutes**

Serves 6

1 tablespoon olive oil

2 slices bacon, diced

1 small yellow onion, peeled and diced

3 cloves garlic, peeled and minced

1 pound egg noodles

Water

2 cups sliced white mushrooms

2 tablespoons gluten-free all-purpose flour

½ cup whole milk

1 teaspoon salt

½ teaspoon ground black pepper

1 tablespoon dried thyme leaves

¼ cup grated Parmesan cheese

2 tablespoons unsalted butter

1 Press the Sauté button on the Instant Pot® and heat oil 30 seconds. Add bacon and onion to pot and stir-fry 5 minutes until onions are translucent. Add garlic and cook for an additional minute.

2 Place egg noodles in an even layer in the Instant Pot®. Pour enough water to come about ¼" above noodles. Add mushrooms. Lock lid.

3 Press the Manual or Pressure Cook button and adjust cook time to 2 minutes. When timer beeps, let pressure release naturally for 3 minutes. Quick-release any additional pressure until float valve drops and unlock lid. Drain any extra liquid.

4 While noodles are cooking, whisk together flour, milk, salt, pepper, thyme, and Parmesan cheese in a small bowl. Set aside.

5 Pour mixture from small bowl over noodles and stir. Add butter. Press the Sauté button on the Instant Pot®, then press Adjust button to change temperature to Less, and simmer unlidded 2 minutes to thicken sauce. Stir.

6 Transfer mixture to a serving dish and serve warm.

Butter and Parsley Egg Noodles

Buttered egg noodles are comforting, as they take many of us back to childhood. In addition, the silkiness of the egg noodles is complemented by the luxuriousness of the butter. To step things up, invest in some pure Irish butter. Using good-quality butter with those silky noodles, this dish showcases the fact that uncomplicated food with top-of-the-line ingredients is simply the best.

- **Hands-On Time: 5 minutes**
- **Cook Time: 4 minutes**

Serves 4

1 pound egg noodles
Water
3 tablespoons unsalted butter
1 tablespoon gluten-free all-purpose flour
¼ cup chopped fresh parsley
1 teaspoon salt
½ teaspoon ground black pepper

1 Place egg noodles in an even layer in the Instant Pot®. Add enough water to come ¼" over noodles. Lock lid.

2 Press the Manual or Pressure Cook button and adjust cook time to 2 minutes. When timer beeps, let pressure release naturally for 3 minutes. Quick-release any additional pressure until float valve drops and unlock lid. Reserve 2 tablespoons of liquid from pot and drain remaining liquid.

3 Add reserved pot liquid, butter, flour, parsley, salt, and pepper to pot. Press the Sauté button on the Instant Pot®, then press Adjust button to change temperature to Less, and simmer unlidded 2 minutes to thicken sauce. Stir.

4 Transfer mixture to a serving dish and serve warm.

Tuna Penne Noodle Casserole

Bring this classic one-dish meal into this century by changing up the noodles and letting your Instant Pot® do all of the work. Read labels, as some canned tuna lists vegetable broth as an ingredient, which actually contains gluten traces. For a change of protein, substitute the tuna with cooked chicken. And, for a little crunch and a lot of fun, serve each dish with crushed potato chips on top!

- **Hands-On Time: 10 minutes**
- **Cook Time: 10 minutes**

Serves 4

12 ounces gluten-free penne pasta

5 cups water

3 tablespoons unsalted butter

½ cup peeled and diced yellow onion

1 stalk celery, diced

1 cup canned sweet peas, drained

1 (6-ounce) can tuna, drained

1 (10.5-ounce) can condensed cream of mushroom soup

⅔ cup whole milk

¼ cup Parmesan cheese

1 Add pasta and water to the Instant Pot®. Lock lid.

2 Press the Manual or Pressure Cook button and adjust cook time to 4 minutes. When timer beeps, let pressure release naturally for 3 minutes. Quick-release any additional pressure until float valve drops and then unlock lid. Drain pasta and set aside.

3 Press the Sauté button on the Instant Pot®. Add butter, onion, and celery to pot and cook 5 minutes until onions are translucent.

4 Add remaining ingredients to pot and stir for 1 minute. Add pasta to pot. Stir until well combined.

5 Transfer mixture to a serving dish and serve warm.

CANNED TUNA

Sustainability is a huge concern for tuna eaters. Research tuna suppliers, as there are vast differences among the brands. Albacore is high in omega-3 fatty acids, but it is a larger fish, so it contains a higher mercury level, while tuna packed in water has fewer calories.

Bacon Mac 'n' Cheese

Add bacon to just about anything, and the yum factor rises instantly. This heavenly mac and cheese recipe is no exception. Although bacon is a naturally gluten-free food, do your research on the companies. Some brands can get cross-contaminated in packing facilities that also work with products containing gluten. Eat this as a side dish or toss in some peas and chicken for a complete one-pot meal.

- **Hands-On Time: 5 minutes**
- **Cook Time: 9 minutes**

Serves 4

4 slices bacon, diced

12 ounces gluten-free elbow macaroni

5 cups water

¼ cup whole milk

¾ cup shredded sharp Cheddar cheese

¼ cup ricotta cheese

1 tablespoon grated Parmesan cheese

¼ teaspoon ground mustard

1 teaspoon salt

½ teaspoon ground black pepper

1 Press the Sauté button on the Instant Pot®. Add bacon to pot and stir-fry 5 minutes until bacon is crisp. Transfer bacon to a small plate lined with a paper towel until ready to use.

2 Add pasta and water to the Instant Pot®. Lock lid.

3 Press the Manual or Pressure Cook button and adjust cook time to 4 minutes. When timer beeps, let pressure release naturally for 3 minutes. Quick-release any additional pressure until float valve drops and then unlock lid. Drain pasta and set aside.

4 Add milk, all cheeses, ground mustard, salt, and pepper to pot. Add pasta and toss until well combined. Stir in bacon.

5 Transfer mixture to a serving dish and serve warm.

Lemon Herbed Pasta

This fresh and light side tastes great with many entrées. The lemon and herbs are an excellent burst of flavor, pairing nicely with seafood, chicken, or a plate full of grilled veggies. Not all gluten-free pastas taste the same, so do a little at-home taste test until you and your family find a winner. Some may seem a little chewy, while with others you can't tell a difference between them and "real" pasta.

- **Hands-On Time: 5 minutes**
- **Cook Time: 4 minutes**

Serves 4

12 ounces gluten-free fusilli pasta

5 cups water

2 tablespoons unsalted butter

2 tablespoons Parmesan cheese

2 tablespoons lemon juice

1 tablespoon lemon zest

½ teaspoon salt

¼ cup chopped fresh parsley

1 Add pasta and water to the Instant Pot®. Lock lid.

2 Press the Manual or Pressure Cook button and adjust cook time to 4 minutes. When timer beeps, let pressure release naturally for 3 minutes. Quick-release any additional pressure until float valve drops and then unlock lid. Drain pasta and set aside.

3 Add remaining ingredients to pasta and toss until blended. Serve warm.

WHAT IS LEMON ZEST?

Lemon zest is the scrapings collected from the rinds of lemons. Although zest can be purchased in jars and kept in your pantry, there is nothing like the freshly yielded zest of a humble little lemon (or lime or orange!). There are many inexpensive zesters you can purchase—heck, you can even use a paring knife— but whichever you choose, go shallow in the fruit. You want to avoid the bitter white pith hiding underneath the vibrant skin.

Minty Pea Risotto

Listen—can you hear that? This side dish is screaming for a lamb chop! Mint and lamb go together like bacon and eggs. But there's no need to limit this versatile, delicious recipe: it is also an ideal complement for shrimp, fish, or a big, juicy steak!

- **Hands-On Time: 5 minutes**
- **Cook Time: 21 minutes**

Serves 4

4 tablespoons unsalted butter

2 medium shallots, peeled and diced

2 cloves garlic, peeled and minced

1½ cups Arborio rice

4 cups chicken broth, divided

½ teaspoon salt

¼ teaspoon ground black pepper

1 teaspoon lime zest

¾ cup chopped fresh mint leaves

1 cup fresh or frozen peas

1 Press the Sauté button on the Instant Pot®. Add butter to pot and heat 30 seconds until melted. Add shallots and stir-fry 5 minutes until they are translucent. Add garlic and rice and cook for an additional minute.

2 Add 1 cup broth and stir 3 minutes until it is absorbed by rice. Add remaining 3 cups broth, salt, and pepper. Lock lid.

3 Press the Manual or Pressure Cook button and adjust cook time to 10 minutes. When timer beeps, let pressure release naturally for 10 minutes. Quick-release any additional pressure until float valve drops and then unlock lid.

4 Stir in lime zest, mint, and peas. Heat 3 minutes until peas are heated through.

5 Ladle risotto into four bowls and serve warm.

Tuna Pasta Salad

Make this recipe on your prep day, portioning it into individual containers for quick-grab meals. Being prepared when abiding by special diet requirements helps ensure that you stay on track and keeps you from having to find quick takeout that is not only gluten-free but healthy. This salad is superquick to put together and actually tastes better the next day or so because the flavors have had a chance to marry together.

- **Hands-On Time: 10 minutes**
- **Cook Time: 4 minutes**

Serves 4

12 ounces gluten-free elbow macaroni

5 cups water

2 (5-ounce) cans of tuna, drained

2 tablespoons dill pickle relish

½ teaspoon dill pickle relish juice

½ cup mayonnaise

2 teaspoons yellow mustard

¼ cup canned sweet peas, drained

½ teaspoon salt

½ teaspoon ground black pepper

1 Add pasta and water to the Instant Pot®. Lock lid.

2 Press the Manual or Pressure Cook button and adjust cook time to 4 minutes. When timer beeps, let pressure release naturally for 3 minutes. Quick-release any additional pressure until float valve drops and then unlock lid. Drain pasta and set aside.

3 Add remaining ingredients to pasta and toss until blended.

4 Refrigerate salad in a lidded container 60 minutes or up to overnight and serve chilled.

Heavenly Prosciutto Risotto

The Instant Pot® was obviously made for risotto lovers. No longer do you have to stand over a skillet stirring constantly. Now you can get a delicious homemade meal on the table and still do everything else you need to do, all without breaking a sweat. Those folks who turn their noses up to gluten-free dishes have certainly never tried the endless options... especially risotto!

- **Hands-On Time: 5 minutes**
- **Cook Time: 14 minutes**

Serves 4

4 tablespoons unsalted butter

2 cloves garlic, peeled and minced

1½ cups Arborio rice

4 cups chicken broth, divided

¼ cup grated Parmesan cheese

½ teaspoon salt

¼ teaspoon ground black pepper

4 ounces prosciutto, ripped into bite-sized pieces

½ cup chopped fresh parsley

1 Press the Sauté button on the Instant Pot®. Add butter to pot and heat 30 seconds until melted. Add garlic and stir-fry 1 minute until garlic starts to soften. Keep a close eye so as not to burn the garlic.

2 Add rice and 1 cup broth to pot and stir for 3 minutes until broth is absorbed by rice.

3 Add remaining 3 cups broth, Parmesan cheese, salt, and pepper to pot. Lock lid.

4 Press the Manual or Pressure Cook button and adjust cook time to 10 minutes. When timer beeps, let pressure release naturally for 10 minutes. Quick-release any additional pressure until float valve drops and then unlock lid.

5 Ladle risotto into four bowls and garnish with prosciutto and parsley. Serve warm.

WHY IS ARBORIO RICE USED IN RISOTTO?

Arborio rice is a short-grain rice that is less milled, leaving it with less structure. This produces a starchier product, thereby lending a smooth risotto if prepared properly. Although a long-grain rice can be used as a substitute, the final result will not have that supercreamy result that Arborio yields.

Tomato, Basil, and Ricotta Risotto

Arborio rice makes a silky risotto because of its high rice gluten, but don't worry; rice gluten is completely different from the "bad" wheat gluten. The added dollop of ricotta cheese, along with tomato paste and fresh basil, creates a dish that is over-the-top in flavor.

- **Hands-On Time: 5 minutes**
- **Cook Time: 13 minutes**

Serves 4

4 tablespoons unsalted butter
4 cups chicken broth, divided
1½ cups Arborio rice
2 tablespoons tomato paste
½ teaspoon salt
¼ teaspoon ground black pepper
¼ cup ricotta cheese
¼ cup julienned fresh basil leaves

1 Press the Sauté button on the Instant Pot®. Add butter to pot and heat 30 seconds until melted.

2 Add 1 cup broth and rice. Stir 3 minutes until broth is absorbed by rice. Add remaining 3 cups broth, tomato paste, salt, and pepper. Lock lid.

3 Press the Manual or Pressure Cook button and adjust cook time to 10 minutes. When timer beeps, let pressure release naturally for 10 minutes. Quick-release any additional pressure until float valve drops and then unlock lid. Gently fold in ricotta cheese.

4 Ladle risotto into four bowls, garnish with basil, and serve warm.

Yellow Basmati Rice

Much healthier than the preservative-filled options at the grocery store, serve this recipe with a nice fish or chicken dish and a side salad or steamed broccoli.

- **Hands-On Time: 5 minutes**
- **Cook Time: 8 minutes**

Serves 8

2 tablespoons unsalted butter
¼ cup peeled and diced yellow onion
2 cups basmati rice
2 cups chicken broth
1 teaspoon ground turmeric
⅛ teaspoon salt

1 Press the Sauté button on the Instant Pot®. Add butter to pot and heat 30 seconds until melted. Add onion and cook 5 minutes until onions are translucent. Add remaining ingredients. Lock lid.

2 Press the Manual or Pressure Cook button and adjust cook time to 3 minutes. When timer beeps, let pressure release naturally for 5 minutes. Quick-release any additional pressure until float valve drops and then unlock lid.

3 Ladle rice into eight bowls and serve warm.

California Roll Sushi Bowl

Eating sushi while on a gluten-free diet can be tricky. We know that soy sauce is a no-no, but did you know that the crab used in most sushi rolls is imitation crab that contains wheat? And, though rice is gluten-free, some of the rice wines and vinegars that make the rice in sushi "sticky" may contain gluten as well. So, if you're craving a little sushi but don't want the hassle of researching what is actually 100 percent gluten-free, make this sushi bowl yourself and know exactly what the ingredients contain!

- **Hands-On Time: 5 minutes**
- **Cook Time: 14 minutes**

Serves 4

Sushi Rice

2 cups sushi rice
2 cups water
¼ cup apple cider vinegar
1 tablespoon granulated sugar
½ teaspoon salt

Toppings

1 avocado, peeled, pitted, and diced
2 medium carrots, peeled and cut into sticks
1 cup peeled and diced cucumbers
½ pound lump crabmeat
4 teaspoons grated fresh gingerroot
4 teaspoons black sesame seeds
2 nori sheets, crumbled
¼ cup tamari

Wasabi Dressing

¼ cup mayonnaise
1 tablespoon minced horseradish root
1 tablespoon lime juice

1 Rinse sushi rice several times through a sieve until water runs clear. Add rice and water to the Instant Pot®. Lock lid.

2 Press the Rice button and cook 12 minutes. When timer beeps, let pressure release naturally for 10 minutes. Quick-release any additional pressure until float valve drops and then unlock lid.

3 While rice is cooking, add vinegar, sugar, and salt to a small saucepan on the stovetop. Over medium-high heat, stir 2 minutes until sugar and salt dissolve. Add mixture to rice and toss.

4 Transfer rice to four bowls. Add avocado, carrots, cucumbers, crabmeat, gingerroot, and sesame seeds. Top with crumbled nori and drizzle with tamari.

5 Whisk together dressing ingredients and drizzle over sushi bowls. Serve.

Wild Rice with Shiitake Mushrooms

All mushroom varieties can be used in this dish; however, the smokiness and unique buttery flavor of the shiitakes pair perfectly with the wild rice. If you can't find fresh shiitakes, look for the dehydrated variety and soak them in water 30 minutes to rehydrate before using.

- **Hands-On Time: 5 minutes**
- **Cook Time: 8 minutes**

Serves 4

1 cup wild rice, rinsed

1½ cups chicken broth

2 teaspoons salt

2 tablespoons unsalted butter

1 cup chopped shiitakes

1 tablespoon tamari

4 scallions, whites and greens, sliced and divided

1 Place rice, broth, and salt into the Instant Pot®. Lock lid.

2 Press the Manual or Pressure Cook button and adjust cook time to 3 minutes. When timer beeps, let pressure release naturally for 5 minutes. Quick-release any additional pressure until float valve drops and then unlock lid. Transfer rice to a bowl and set aside.

3 Press the Sauté button on the Instant Pot®. Add butter, shiitakes, tamari, and the whites of scallions. Stir-fry 4 minutes until scallions become translucent. Add rice to pot. Stir and heat for an additional minute.

4 Transfer rice to four bowls. Garnish with scallion greens and serve warm.

Greek "Fried" Rice

The explosion of flavors in this dish ranges from the brininess of the olives and soothing freshness of the cucumbers to the tanginess of the feta cheese. Serve this side dish with lamb kebabs, tzatziki sauce, and freshly sliced tomatoes for a tasty gluten-free Greek dining experience.

- **Hands-On Time: 10 minutes**
- **Cook Time: 5 minutes**

Serves 4

1 cup long-grain white rice

1 (14.5-ounce) can diced tomatoes, including juice

¼ cup water

1 teaspoon salt

2 large eggs, whisked

½ cup peeled and seeded diced English cucumber

¼ cup crumbled feta cheese

¼ cup sliced Kalamata olives

¼ cup chopped fresh mint leaves

1 Place rice, tomatoes with juice, water, and salt in the Instant Pot®. Lock lid.

2 Press the Manual or Pressure Cook button and adjust cook time to 3 minutes. When timer beeps, let pressure release naturally for 10 minutes. Quick-release any additional pressure until float valve drops and then unlock lid.

3 Make a well in the middle of the rice and add whisked eggs to well. Stir eggs into rice and stir-fry 2 minutes.

4 Transfer rice mixture to a serving dish. Toss in cucumber, feta cheese, and olives. Garnish with mint leaves and serve warm.

7

Poultry Main Dishes

This chapter covers birds such as duck, Cornish hen, turkey, and chicken (which is probably one of the most consumed proteins in the United States). There are so many gluten-free recipes out there and a handful of go-to meals that you can cook for your family, but if you're sick of eating dried-out chicken breasts and overcooked thighs, the Instant Pot® is your new best friend. The steam and pressure used to cook ingredients in the pot are guaranteed to leave the chicken dishes in this chapter juicy and delicious. Whether you're craving a Chicken Fajita Bowl or Citrus Honey Chicken Legs, or your family is calling for Buffalo Chicken Tostados or Renaissance Festival Turkey Legs, you'll find a new favorite recipe in this chapter!

Also, if you're planning on getting home late, the Instant Pot® allows you to start a meal in the morning and set it to automatically switch to the Keep Warm function for up to 10 hours, which means dinner will be ready and waiting when you walk in the door. So, go get cookin'!

Herb Roasted Whole Chicken

Sure, you can pick up a precooked chicken at the supermarket, but why not cook your own, so you can control the ingredients and seasonings and achieve moist and tender chicken with ease in the Instant Pot®? If you prefer a little crispiness on the outside chicken skin, you can finish the chicken off in the oven. Speaking of crispiness, be warned that several grocers add a little gluten flour to the skin of the chicken to give it an extra-crispy exterior.

- **Hands-On Time: 10 minutes**
- **Cook Time: 25 minutes**

Serves 4

1 teaspoon dried thyme
    leaves
1 teaspoon dried oregano
    leaves
1 teaspoon dried basil leaves
1 teaspoon garlic powder
1 teaspoon salt
1 teaspoon ground black
    pepper
1 tablespoon olive oil
1 (5-pound) whole chicken
1 small red apple, peeled,
    cored, and quartered
1 medium sweet onion,
    peeled and roughly
    chopped, divided
3 cloves garlic, peeled and
    halved
2 cups water

1 In a small bowl, combine thyme, oregano, basil, garlic powder, salt, and pepper.

2 Brush oil on the outside of chicken. Sprinkle mixture from small bowl evenly over chicken. Place apple quarters and half of onion in the cavity of the bird.

3 Add remaining onion and garlic to the Instant Pot®. Add water to pot. Insert steam rack over vegetables. Place chicken on steam rack. Lock lid.

4 Press the Manual or Pressure Cook button and adjust cook time to 25 minutes. When timer beeps, let pressure release naturally until float valve drops and then unlock lid. Check chicken using a meat thermometer to ensure the internal temperature is at least 165°F.

5 Transfer chicken to a cutting board and discard apple and onion from the chicken cavity. Let chicken rest for 5 minutes until cool enough to carve. Serve warm.

Chicken Fajita Bowl

This mouthwatering bowl is filled with healthy ingredients and explodes with flavor. It's also free from cross contamination. Mexican restaurants can be a minefield when you're trying to navigate options: from the deep fryer to the gluten-laced sauces and queso, eating gluten-free may be challenging. Although this ingredient list looks rather long, a lot of these items are already in your pantry, and the others are fairly inexpensive.

- **Hands-On Time: 15 minutes**
- **Cook Time: 5 minutes**

Serves 4

Chicken

2 tablespoons olive oil

Zest of 1 lime

Juice of 1 lime

1 teaspoon salt

½ teaspoon ground black pepper

1 tablespoon chili powder

1 tablespoon ground cumin

⅛ teaspoon red pepper flakes

1 pound boneless, skinless chicken breasts, cut into 1" cubes

1 small green bell pepper, seeded and sliced

1 small red bell pepper, seeded and sliced

1 small yellow bell pepper, seeded and sliced

1 small sweet onion, peeled and sliced

½ cup water

Bowl Ingredients

1 avocado, peeled, pitted, and diced

2 Roma tomatoes, seeded and diced

½ cup sour cream

1 cup shredded Cheddar cheese

1 In a medium bowl, whisk together olive oil, lime zest, lime juice, salt, pepper, chili powder, cumin, and red pepper flakes. Add chicken, bell pepper slices, and onion. Toss and refrigerate at least 30 minutes or up to overnight.

2 Add water and chicken mixture to the Instant Pot®. Lock lid.

3 Press the Manual or Pressure Cook button and adjust cook time to 5 minutes. When timer beeps, let pressure release naturally for 10 minutes. Quick-release any additional pressure until float valve drops and then unlock lid. Check chicken using a meat thermometer to ensure the internal temperature is at least 165°F.

4 Using a slotted spoon, transfer chicken and veggie mixture to four bowls.

5 Garnish with avocado, tomatoes, sour cream, and Cheddar cheese. Serve warm.

Caprese Chicken Bowl

This dish is a play on the very fresh Insalata Caprese, traditionally made with buffalo mozzarella, a semisoft cheese that has been replicated using cow's milk and is readily available at most grocers. Of course, those basic rectangles of mozzarella cheese may also be used in this chicken bowl; however, the moist, round variety is the way to go!

- **Hands-On Time: 5 minutes**
- **Cook Time: 5 minutes**

Serves 4

1½ **pounds boneless, skinless chicken breasts, cut into 1" cubes**

1 **(28-ounce) can diced tomatoes, including juice**

1 **(8-ounce) ball fresh mozzarella, cubed**

1 **tablespoon olive oil**

½ **teaspoon salt**

½ **teaspoon ground black pepper**

½ **cup julienned fresh basil leaves**

1 Add chicken and tomatoes with juice to the Instant Pot®. Lock lid.

2 Press the Manual or Pressure Cook button and adjust cook time to 5 minutes. When timer beeps, let pressure release naturally for 10 minutes. Quick-release any additional pressure until float valve drops and then unlock lid. Check chicken using a meat thermometer to ensure the internal temperature is at least 165°F.

3 Using a slotted spoon, transfer chicken and tomatoes to four bowls. Garnish chicken with mozzarella cubes. Drizzle with olive oil. Season with salt, pepper, and basil, and serve.

Easy Salsa Chicken

With the vast supply of salsas on the shelves of grocery stores, this recipe can be different every time you make it. Whether it be mild tomato salsa or spicy peach salsa, the possibilities for this dish are almost endless. Also, if you don't have fresh gluten-free broth on hand, just use water. It won't infuse quite as much flavor, but it will do the trick for a meal at the last minute.

- **Hands-On Time: 5 minutes**
- **Cook Time: 5 minutes**

Serves 4

1½ **pounds boneless, skinless chicken breasts, cut into 1" cubes**
1 **(16-ounce) jar salsa**
½ **cup chicken broth**

1 Add chicken, salsa, and broth to the Instant Pot®. Lock lid.

2 Press the Manual or Pressure Cook button and adjust cook time to 5 minutes. When timer beeps, let pressure release naturally for 10 minutes. Quick-release any additional pressure until float valve drops and then unlock lid. Check chicken using a meat thermometer to ensure the internal temperature is at least 165°F.

3 Transfer chicken and salsa to a serving dish and serve warm.

Citrus Honey Chicken Legs

Instead of serving that bucket of fried chicken where everyone fights for the legs, why not make a meal that is only the legs? In addition to keeping the peace at the dinner table, this chicken is cheaper, healthier, and yummier! The tang and sweetness is accented with the small addition of cayenne and ginger, lending a hint of Thai flavor that is sure to please your hungry group. Even the gluten-lovers won't be able to tell that these legs are gluten-free!

- **Hands-On Time: 10 minutes**
- **Cook Time: 15 minutes**

Serves 4

Juice of 1 medium orange
Juice of 1 small lime
1 teaspoon orange zest
½ cup honey
1 tablespoon tamari
½ teaspoon cayenne pepper
¼ teaspoon ground ginger
1 teaspoon salt
2 pounds chicken legs
1 cup water

WHAT IS TAMARI?

Tamari is a gluten-free soy sauce. Make sure you read your labels and see the words *gluten-free*. Some brands of tamari do have trace amounts of wheat.

1 In a large bowl, combine orange juice, lime juice, zest, honey, tamari, cayenne pepper, ground ginger, and salt. Set aside ¼ cup of the mixture. Add chicken legs to the bowl and toss. Refrigerate at least 30 minutes or up to overnight.

2 Add water to the Instant Pot® and insert steam rack. Press the Adjust button and change temperature to Less. Arrange chicken standing up, meaty side down, on the steam rack. Lock lid.

3 Press the Poultry button and cook for the default time of 15 minutes. When timer beeps, quick-release pressure until float valve drops and then unlock lid. Check chicken using a meat thermometer to ensure the internal temperature is at least 165°F.

4 Transfer chicken to a serving dish. Brush with reserved sauce. Serve warm.

Korean Gochujang Chicken Legs

Gochujang is the "it" sauce of late. A fermented red chili paste, this sweet and spicy condiment is all the rage. Be sure to read your labels. Some commercially produced gochujang contains seed malt, which is a derivative of barley. There are gluten-free brands available, as well as many recipes if you want to take the homemade approach. Gochujang is great in chilis, soups, sauces, and marinades, so you won't have to worry about using it once and then adding it to the condiment graveyard in your refrigerator.

- **Hands-On Time: 10 minutes**
- **Cook Time: 15 minutes**

Serves 4

¼ cup gluten-free gochujang sauce

2 tablespoons rice vinegar

2 tablespoons honey

1 tablespoon tamari

2 cloves garlic, peeled and quartered

1" knob fresh ginger, scrubbed and sliced

2 pounds chicken legs

1 cup water

2 tablespoons toasted sesame seeds

¼ cup chopped fresh cilantro

1 In a large bowl, combine gochujang, rice vinegar, honey, tamari, garlic, and ginger. Set aside ¼ cup of mixture. Add chicken legs to the bowl and toss. Cover and refrigerate at least 30 minutes or up to overnight.

2 Add water to the Instant Pot® and insert steam rack. Press the Adjust button and change temperature to Less. Arrange chicken standing up, meaty side down, on the steam rack. Lock lid.

3 Press the Poultry button and cook for the default time of 15 minutes. When timer beeps, quick-release pressure until float valve drops and then unlock lid. Check chicken using a meat thermometer to ensure the internal temperature is at least 165°F.

4 Transfer chicken to a serving dish. Brush with reserved sauce and garnish with sesame seeds and cilantro. Serve warm.

Bite-Sized Chicken Cacciatore

In Italy, a meal served with the designation *cacciatore* translates to being prepared "hunter-style." It is straightforward in preparation, using onions, bell peppers, tomatoes, and wine, along with fragrant herbs. Although the ingredients are simple, the symphony of flavors in this dish is heaven, proving that simple ingredients don't have to be simple in taste.

- **Hands-On Time: 15 minutes**
- **Cook Time: 23 minutes**

Serves 4

1 tablespoon olive oil

1 small yellow onion, peeled and diced

1 green bell pepper, seeded and diced

2 cups quartered white mushrooms

4 cloves garlic, peeled and minced

½ cup dry white wine

2 pounds boneless, skinless chicken thighs, cut into 1" cubes

1 (28-ounce) can fire-roasted diced tomatoes, including juice

½ cup chicken broth

2 tablespoons capers, drained

1 teaspoon caper juice (from the jar)

1 tablespoon Italian seasoning

½ teaspoon ground black pepper

¼ cup chopped fresh basil leaves

¼ cup grated Parmesan cheese

1 Press the Sauté button on the Instant Pot® and heat oil 30 seconds. Add onion, bell pepper, and mushrooms to pot. Sauté for 5 minutes until onions are translucent. Add garlic and heat an additional 1 minute.

2 Add wine to pot and stir. Heat for 2 minutes to allow alcohol to cook off. Add chicken, tomatoes with juice, broth, capers, caper juice, Italian seasoning, and black pepper. Lock lid.

3 Press the Poultry button and cook for the default time of 15 minutes. When timer beeps, let pressure release naturally for 5 minutes. Quick-release any additional pressure until float valve drops and then unlock lid. Check chicken using a meat thermometer to ensure the internal temperature is at least 165°F.

4 Using a slotted spoon, transfer chicken to four bowls and garnish with fresh basil and Parmesan cheese. Serve warm.

Cajun Chicken Legs

The aromatics of these simple chicken legs will fill your kitchen with love—for the chicken *and* for the chef! There are a variety of Cajun seasoning mixes to choose from, so just look at the ingredients and pick your favorite. Be careful here: the seasonings alone are gluten-free, but some brands will add fillers or anti-clumping ingredients to their seasoning mixes. There are several gluten-free Cajun seasonings available, as well as many homemade versions.

- **Hands-On Time: 10 minutes**
- **Cook Time: 15 minutes**

Serves 4

1 tablespoon gluten-free Cajun seasoning

1 tablespoon Dijon mustard

1 tablespoon vegetable oil

1 tablespoon light brown sugar

⅛ teaspoon cayenne pepper

2 pounds chicken legs

1 cup water

1 In a large bowl, combine Cajun seasoning, mustard, oil, brown sugar, and cayenne pepper. Set aside ¼ cup of mixture. Add chicken legs to the bowl and toss. Refrigerate covered at least 30 minutes or up to overnight.

2 Add water to the Instant Pot® and insert steam rack. Press the Adjust button and change temperature to Less. Arrange chicken standing up, meaty side down, on the steam rack. Lock lid.

3 Press the Poultry button and cook for the default time of 15 minutes. When timer beeps, quick-release pressure until float valve drops and then unlock lid. Check chicken using a meat thermometer to ensure the internal temperature is at least 165°F.

4 Transfer chicken to a serving dish. Brush with reserved sauce and serve warm.

Chicken Thighs with Island Salsa

This is the perfect summer meal to enjoy alfresco with a light and crisp glass of Chardonnay, although it is equally enjoyable packed as a picnic with a jug of sun tea! If you prepare the salsa ahead of time, make sure to toss in the avocado right before serving to avoid browning.

- **Hands-On Time: 5 minutes**
- **Cook Time: 7 minutes**

Serves 8

Island Salsa

½ cup diced peeled pineapple

½ cup diced peeled mango

½ cup fresh lime juice

1 tablespoon lime zest

1 Roma tomato, seeded and diced

¼ cup peeled and finely diced red onion

1 medium avocado, peeled, pitted, and diced

¼ cup chopped fresh cilantro

¼ cup chopped fresh mint leaves

1 teaspoon salt

Chicken

3 pounds boneless, skinless chicken thighs

1 teaspoon salt

½ teaspoon ground black pepper

1 cup water

FRUIT SALSA TIP

Grill your fruit before dicing it. The heat will caramelize the natural sugars in the fruit and lend a completely different and sweet flavor note to your salsa.

1 In a large bowl, combine pineapple, mango, lime juice, lime zest, tomato, onion, avocado, cilantro, mint, and salt. Refrigerate salsa covered at least 1 hour or up to overnight.

2 Pat chicken thighs dry with a paper towel. Season with salt and pepper.

3 Add water to the Instant Pot® and insert steam rack. Place steamer basket on the steam rack. Arrange thighs evenly in steamer basket. Lock lid.

4 Press the Manual or Pressure Cook button and adjust cook time to 7 minutes. When timer beeps, quick-release pressure until float valve drops and then unlock lid. Check chicken using a meat thermometer to ensure the internal temperature is at least 165°F.

5 Transfer chicken to eight plates. Garnish with salsa and serve.

Artichoke Hearts and Chicken Thighs

The unique brininess of the artichokes coupled with the juiciness of the chicken thighs are a great pairing and can be served alone or atop rice or gluten-free pasta.

- **Hands-On Time: 5 minutes**
- **Cook Time: 7 minutes**

Serves 8

1 teaspoon sea salt

1 teaspoon smoked paprika

½ teaspoon ground black pepper

3 pounds boneless, skinless chicken thighs

½ cup water

2 (6.5-ounce) jars marinated artichoke hearts, undrained

½ cup chopped fresh parsley

1 In a medium bowl, combine salt, smoked paprika, and pepper. Add chicken and toss. Refrigerate covered at least 30 minutes or up to overnight.

2 Add chicken, water, and artichoke hearts with juice to the Instant Pot®. Lock lid.

3 Press the Manual or Pressure Cook button and adjust cook time to 7 minutes. When timer beeps, quick-release pressure until float valve drops and then unlock lid. Check chicken using a meat thermometer to ensure the internal temperature is at least 165°F.

4 Using a slotted spoon, transfer chicken and artichokes to serving dish. Garnish with parsley and serve.

Persian Chicken

Although each culture has spices specific to its different regions, Persian culture rules the spice world with extensive marketplaces showcasing the colorful array of choices. This chicken dish proves that the sum is greater than its parts by infusing some common spices like nutmeg, cinnamon, turmeric, and cumin, blending them together to create a delicious, lip-smacking meal.

- **Hands-On Time: 5 minutes**
- **Cook Time: 7 minutes**

Serves 6

1 tablespoon honey
1 tablespoon olive oil
1 teaspoon lime zest
3 cloves garlic, peeled and quartered
1 teaspoon turmeric
1 teaspoon ground cinnamon
½ teaspoon ground cumin
⅛ teaspoon ground nutmeg
⅛ teaspoon allspice
½ teaspoon salt
¼ teaspoon ground black pepper
3 pounds boneless, skinless chicken thighs
1 cup water
1 lime, quartered

1. In a medium bowl, combine honey, olive oil, lime zest, garlic, turmeric, cinnamon, cumin, nutmeg, allspice, salt, and pepper. Add chicken thighs and toss. Refrigerate covered at least 1 hour or up to overnight.

2. Add water to the Instant Pot® and insert steamer basket. Arrange thighs evenly in steamer basket. Lock lid.

3. Press the Manual or Pressure Cook button and adjust cook time to 7 minutes. When timer beeps, quick-release pressure until float valve drops and then unlock lid. Check chicken using a meat thermometer to ensure the internal temperature is at least 165°F.

4. Transfer chicken thighs to serving dish and garnish with lime. Serve warm.

Buffalo Chicken Tostados

These Buffalo Chicken Tostados are a great twist on a bar menu classic. Make them for dinner and then pack one for lunch the next day. If you're serving a crowd, just double or triple the recipe to make sure all your guests get their share! Also, offer both flour and corn tortillas as an option for your gluten-loving guests.

- **Hands-On Time: 10 minutes**
- **Cook Time: 15 minutes**

Yields 8 tostados

2 cups buffalo wing sauce

2 tablespoons unsalted butter, melted

2 pounds boneless, skinless chicken breasts, halved

8 corn tostados

1 cup finely diced celery

1 large carrot, peeled and grated

1 cup crumbled blue cheese

1 In a large bowl, whisk together wing sauce and butter. Add chicken breasts and toss until coated. Place chicken and sauce in the Instant Pot®. Lock lid.

2 Press the Manual or Pressure Cook button and adjust cook time to 15 minutes. When timer beeps, let pressure release naturally for 10 minutes. Quick-release any additional pressure until float valve drops and then unlock lid. Check chicken using a meat thermometer to ensure the internal temperature is at least 165°F.

3 Use two forks to pull chicken apart in the Instant Pot®; mix with juices in pot.

4 Using a slotted spoon, place ⅛ of chicken mixture on each tostado. Garnish each with celery, carrot, and blue cheese. Serve warm.

Chicken and Green Olives

Don't throw away the juice from that jar of olives after the olives are gone. It is a simple salted vinegar solution, but it has been enhanced by the olives, creating a beautiful brine for the chicken in this recipe. It is also tasty in pasta sauces, vinaigrettes, and even mayonnaise when creating a flavored aioli for an artisan sandwich on gluten-free bread.

- **Hands-On Time: 10 minutes**
- **Cook Time: 8 minutes**

Serves 4

2 tablespoons olive oil

1 tablespoon tomato paste

¼ cup Manzanilla green olive juice (from the jar of olives)

1 tablespoon Dijon mustard

1 teaspoon Italian seasoning

1 teaspoon minced fresh garlic

1½ pounds boneless, skinless chicken thighs, cut into 1" cubes

1 cup water

½ cup halved Manzanilla green olives

2 tablespoons fresh thyme leaves

½ teaspoon ground black pepper

2 tablespoons gluten-free all-purpose flour

1 In a medium bowl, whisk together olive oil, tomato paste, olive juice, Dijon mustard, Italian seasoning, and garlic. Add chicken, toss, and refrigerate at least 30 minutes or up to overnight.

2 Add water and chicken mixture, including marinade, to the Instant Pot®. Lock lid.

3 Press the Manual or Pressure Cook button and adjust cook time to 6 minutes. When timer beeps, let the pressure release naturally for 10 minutes. Quick-release any additional pressure until float valve drops and then unlock lid. Check chicken using a meat thermometer to ensure the internal temperature is at least 165°F. Stir in olives, thyme, and pepper.

4 Using a slotted spoon, transfer chicken and olives to a serving bowl.

5 Whisk flour into pot juices and cook 2 minutes until mixture thickens. Ladle mixture over chicken and serve warm.

Chicken Cordon Bleu

This is an oldie but goodie that just got a face-lift from the Instant Pot®. If you can't find any gluten-free bread crumbs, pulse some oats in a food processor and use as a substitute. There are also rice panko bread crumbs found in the Asian section of the grocery store for another gluten-free option.

- **Hands-On Time: 15 minutes**
- **Cook Time: 15 minutes**

Serves 4

- 4 boneless, skinless chicken breasts, halved
- 1½ cups gluten-free bread crumbs
- 1 tablespoon Italian seasoning
- 1 teaspoon salt
- ½ teaspoon ground black pepper
- 1 large egg
- 2 tablespoons whole milk
- 2 tablespoons unsalted butter, melted
- 1 tablespoon Dijon mustard
- 4 medium slices deli ham
- 8 thin slices Swiss cheese
- 1½ cups water

1 Place one chicken breast half between two pieces of parchment paper. Using the flat side of a meat tenderizer, pound chicken until it is approximately ½" in thickness. Repeat with remaining chicken.

2 In a large bowl, combine bread crumbs, Italian seasoning, salt, and pepper. Set aside. In a medium bowl, whisk together egg and milk. Set aside.

3 In a small bowl, combine melted butter and Dijon mustard. Brush one side of chicken with mixture. Layer brushed chicken with one slice ham and two slices Swiss cheese. Roll chicken up tightly. Set aside seam side down. Repeat with remaining chicken.

4 Dip each rolled chicken breast in egg mixture and then dredge in bread crumb mixture. Place breasts in steamer basket.

5 Add water to the Instant Pot®. Insert steamer basket and place stuffed chicken in basket. Lock lid.

6 Press the Manual or Pressure Cook button and adjust cook time to 10 minutes. When timer beeps, let pressure release naturally for 10 minutes. Quick-release any additional pressure until float valve drops and then unlock lid. Check chicken using a meat thermometer to ensure the internal temperature is at least 165°F.

7 Preheat oven to broiler for 500°F.

8 Transfer chicken to a baking sheet lined with parchment paper. Broil 5 minutes.

9 Transfer chicken to a cutting board and let rest for 5 minutes. Slice and serve.

Chicken Parmesan Meatballs

Although chicken Parmesan is traditionally made using chicken breasts with mozzarella melted on top, these meatballs are the perfect vessel to deliver a little cheesy surprise on the inside. And instead of those pesky gluten-filled bread crumbs, the cornmeal substitute lends a sweet and rustic component to these meatballs.

- Hands-On Time: 15 minutes
- Cook Time: 28 minutes

Yields 20 meatballs

1 pound ground chicken

2 large eggs

1 tablespoon Italian seasoning

2 tablespoons peeled and finely diced yellow onion

1 teaspoon garlic powder

¼ cup cornmeal

¼ cup grated Parmesan cheese, divided

2 tablespoons plus 2 cups marinara sauce, divided

20 mini mozzarella balls (also called *ciliegine*)

3 tablespoons olive oil, divided

2 cups water

½ cup julienned fresh basil leaves

1 In a medium bowl, combine chicken, eggs, Italian seasoning, onion, garlic powder, cornmeal, half of Parmesan cheese, and 2 tablespoons marinara sauce. Form into 20 meatballs. Press one mozzarella ball into the middle of each meatball.

2 Press the Sauté button on the Instant Pot® and heat 2 tablespoons oil 30 seconds. Place ten meatballs around the edge of pot. Sear meatballs 4 minutes, making sure to get each side. Remove seared meatballs and set aside. Add remaining tablespoon of oil and remaining meatballs and sear 4 minutes.

3 Transfer seared meatballs to a 7-cup glass dish. Top with remaining 2 cups marinara sauce. Discard extra juice and oil from the Instant Pot®.

4 Pour water into the Instant Pot®. Insert steam rack. Place the glass dish on top of the steam rack. Lock lid.

5 Press the Manual or Pressure Cook button and adjust cook time to 20 minutes. When timer beeps, let pressure release naturally for 10 minutes. Quick-release any additional pressure until float valve drops and then unlock lid.

6 Transfer meatballs to a serving dish. Garnish with basil and remaining Parmesan cheese. Serve warm.

Bunless Sloppy Janes

If you want to slop this childhood favorite on a gluten-free bun, go for it, but spooning a few ladles right into a bowl works just as well. The bit of sweetness from the maple syrup is the perfect balance to the multiple savory spices and veggies found in this dish.

- **Hands-On Time: 10 minutes**
- **Cook Time: 4 minutes**

Serves 4

1 tablespoon olive oil

1 pound ground turkey

1 medium yellow onion, peeled and diced

1 small green bell pepper, seeded and diced

1 stalk celery, finely chopped

1 large carrot, scrubbed and grated

2 teaspoons Worcestershire sauce

2 cups tomato sauce

2 tablespoons tomato paste

1 tablespoon pure maple syrup

1 teaspoon salt

1 teaspoon ground black pepper

1 teaspoon smoked paprika

1 Press the Sauté button on the Instant Pot® and heat oil 30 seconds. Add turkey, onion, bell pepper, celery, and carrot. Stir-fry 4 minutes until onions are tender and turkey is mostly browned.

2 Add remaining ingredients to pot. Lock lid.

3 Press the Manual or Pressure Cook button and adjust cook time to 0 minutes. When timer beeps, quick-release pressure until float valve drops and then unlock lid.

4 Transfer mixture to four serving bowls and serve warm.

Skinny Turkey Taco Salad

This taco salad may be light on calories, but it is heavy on flavor. Although the turkey is lean and the yogurt is fat-free, healthy fats are present in the olives and avocado. Don't skip these, as healthy fats are a crucial macronutrient our bodies need to effectively work in conjunction with carbohydrates and proteins. By the way, the healthy carbs in this salad are hiding in the cilantro, bell pepper, and even the tomatoes!

- **Hands-On Time: 15 minutes**
- **Cook Time: 7 minutes**

Serves 4

½ cup fat-free plain Greek yogurt

2 teaspoons sriracha

½ teaspoon salt

Juice from ½ lime

1 tablespoon olive oil

1 medium yellow onion, peeled and diced

1 small green bell pepper, seeded and diced

1 pound lean ground turkey

1 (1.25-ounce) packet gluten-free taco seasoning mix

½ cup water

4 cups shredded iceberg lettuce

¼ cup chopped fresh cilantro

¼ cup shredded Mexican-blend cheese

1 (4.25-ounce) can sliced black olives, drained

1 cup pinto beans, drained and rinsed

1 avocado, peeled, pitted, and diced

2 Roma tomatoes, seeded, diced, and seasoned lightly with salt and pepper

1. In a small bowl, whisk together Greek yogurt, sriracha, salt, and lime juice. Refrigerate covered until ready to use.

2. Press the Sauté button on the Instant Pot® and heat oil 30 seconds. Add onion and bell pepper to pot. Stir-fry 4 minutes until onions are tender. Add turkey and brown for 2 minutes.

3. Stir in taco seasoning mix and water. Lock lid.

4. Press the Manual or Pressure Cook button and adjust cook time to 1 minute. When timer beeps, quick-release pressure until float valve drops and then unlock lid. Stir mixture.

5. Line four bowls with lettuce and cilantro. Using a slotted spoon, transfer cooked turkey mixture to bowls. Garnish with cheese, black olives, pinto beans, avocado, and tomatoes, and drizzle with yogurt dressing. Serve.

Cornish Hens with Ginger-Cherry Glaze

Why is it that a whole chicken is an economical choice, but miniaturized Cornish hens are a sexy meal for two or a fancy dish for guests? Either split the cooked hens in half and serve four guests with a fresh salad and some baked veggies or give everyone a whole hen and go light on the side dishes.

- **Hands-On Time: 10 minutes**
- **Cook Time: 15 minutes**

Serves 2

2 (1½-pound) Cornish hens
¼ cup cherry preserves
1 tablespoon tamari
2 teaspoons ground ginger
1 tablespoon orange zest
1 orange, quartered
1½ cups water

1 Pat down Cornish hens with a paper towel. Set aside.

2 In a small bowl, combine preserves, tamari, ground ginger, and orange zest. Reserve 2 tablespoons of mixture. Rub remaining mixture over Cornish hens. Insert orange quarters into the cavities of the hens.

3 Add water to the Instant Pot®. Insert steamer basket and place hens in basket. Lock lid.

4 Press the Meat button and adjust cook time to 10 minutes. When timer beeps, let pressure release naturally for 5 minutes. Quick-release any additional pressure until float valve drops and then unlock lid. Check hens using a meat thermometer to ensure the internal temperature is at least 165°F.

5 Preheat oven to broiler for 500°F.

6 Transfer hens to a baking sheet and brush remaining cherry preserve mixture on hens. Remove and discard orange from cavities of hens. Broil 5 minutes.

7 Transfer hens to a serving dish. Serve warm.

Renaissance Festival Turkey Legs

Love watching knights on horses, making beeswax candles, and listening to strolling musicians? This is the recipe for you! You'll feel like you've stepped into a Renaissance festival with these big, juicy turkey legs. The hint of hot cayenne blended with the sweet ketchup and brown sugar makes for irresistible flavor.

- **Hands-On Time: 5 minutes**
- **Cook Time: 25 minutes**

Serves 2

- **2 tablespoons light brown sugar**
- **2 tablespoons tamari**
- **2 tablespoons ketchup**
- **1 tablespoon olive oil**
- **1 teaspoon garlic powder**
- **¼ teaspoon cayenne pepper**
- **1 teaspoon salt**
- **2 turkey legs**
- **1 cup water**

1 In a gallon-sized plastic storage bag, combine brown sugar, tamari, ketchup, olive oil, garlic powder, cayenne pepper, and salt. Squeeze around the ingredients without spilling until combined. Add turkey legs and seal bag. Refrigerate at least 30 minutes or up to overnight.

2 Add water to the Instant Pot®. Insert steamer basket. Place turkey legs and leftover marinade in basket. Lock lid.

3 Press the Manual or Pressure Cook button and adjust cook time to 20 minutes. When timer beeps, let pressure release naturally for 10 minutes. Quick-release any additional pressure until float valve drops and then unlock lid. Check turkey using a meat thermometer to ensure the internal temperature is at least 165°F.

4 Preheat oven to broiler for 500°F.

5 Transfer legs to a baking sheet lined with parchment paper. Broil 5 minutes. Serve warm.

Duck à l'Orange Breast

Your dinner mate will think you studied for years at Le Cordon Bleu when you serve this classic French dish. In actuality, it will only take you 20 minutes to get this elegant, gluten-free meal onto a plate. And don't forget to score the duck breast, as it helps render off the fat layer while cooking. Bon appétit!

- **Hands-On Time: 10 minutes**
- **Cook Time: 10 minutes**

Serves 2

⅓ **cup freshly squeezed orange juice (approximately 1 orange)**

1 tablespoon orange zest

2 tablespoons honey

1 pound duck breasts (about 2 breasts)

1 teaspoon salt

½ teaspoon ground black pepper

2 teaspoons gluten-free all-purpose flour

HOW DO YOU SCORE A DUCK BREAST AND WHY?

Scoring the duck breast before cooking is essential to the end result. The duck breast has a thick layer of fat between the skin and the actual meat. Scoring this layer allows the fat to render and melt away, leaving that delectable crispy skin. Place breast on a cutting board skin-side up. Score in diagonal lines about ½" apart. Turn breast and do this again, creating a crosshatch pattern. Be careful to slice only the fat layer and not the actual breast meat.

1 In a small bowl, whisk together orange juice, orange zest, and honey. Set aside.

2 Season both sides of duck breasts with salt and pepper. Carefully score duck fat in a crosshatch pattern, making sure to avoid breast meat.

3 Press the Sauté button on the Instant Pot® and place duck breasts fat-side down in pot. Heat 8 minutes. Do not touch duck, as it is rendering off its fat.

4 Transfer duck to a plate. Pour fat except for 1 teaspoon out of pot. Add duck back to pot fat-side up. Add orange juice mixture. Lock lid.

5 Press the Manual or Pressure Cook button and adjust cook time to 2 minutes. Adjust the pressure to Low. When timer beeps, quick-release pressure until float valve drops and then unlock lid.

6 Transfer duck to a cutting board and let rest 5 minutes. Whisk flour into pot juices until thickened.

7 Slice duck and transfer to two plates. Drizzle sauce from pot over duck. Serve warm.

Beef, Pork, and Lamb Main Dishes

If you only used your Instant Pot® for meats, you would still get your money's worth—and more. The steam and pressure can take a seemingly tough and inexpensive piece of meat and make it taste like butter in your mouth. The steam keeps everything moist, and the pressure helps break down some of the fat and the sinewy parts. And the best part? The trapped steam helps create a meat within 30 minutes that tastes like it has been braised for hours, depending on the meat weight.

With recipes ranging from Pork Meatball Bahn Mi and Mexican Flank Steak to Hawaiian Pork and Lamb Keftedes, this chapter will help get you started on some classic Instant Pot® recipes, as well as introduce you to some new gluten-free favorites.

Carolina Dry-Rubbed Pork Ribs

Just like Southern charm, these tender and juicy ribs are a little bit sweet and a little bit sassy. The steam from the Instant Pot® is the perfect complement for these pork ribs, heating them to perfection. You will never cook these tender, fall-off-the-bone ribs any other way after preparing them under pressure. Enjoy!

- **Hands-On Time: 10 minutes**
- **Cook Time: 30 minutes**

Serves 6

1 teaspoon salt

1 teaspoon ground black pepper

1 teaspoon garlic powder

1 teaspoon onion powder

½ teaspoon cayenne pepper

2 teaspoons chili powder

1 tablespoon smoked paprika

2 tablespoons light brown sugar

1 rack pork ribs (approximately 3½ pounds), cut into 2-rib sections

1 cup water

1 In a small bowl, combine salt, pepper, garlic powder, onion powder, cayenne pepper, chili powder, smoked paprika, and brown sugar. Massage mixture into rib sections. Refrigerate ribs covered at least 30 minutes or up to overnight.

2 Add water to the Instant Pot® and insert steamer basket. Arrange ribs standing upright, meaty side facing outward toward the pot walls in basket. Lock lid.

3 Press the Manual or Pressure Cook button and adjust cook time to 30 minutes. When timer beeps, let pressure release naturally until float valve drops and then unlock lid.

4 Transfer ribs to a serving dish and serve warm.

Pork Loin with Creamed Spinach and Blistered Tomatoes

This dish is a perfect example of how inexpensive ingredients can be turned into something special—and even a little sexy. Serve this meal for two by candlelight with mood music in the background, and your special friend will thank you for your excellent chef skills!

- **Hands-On Time: 10 minutes**
- **Cook Time: 17 minutes**

Serves 2

Pork Loin
1 teaspoon salt
1 teaspoon ground black pepper
1 teaspoon Italian seasoning
2 tablespoons all-purpose gluten-free flour
1 tablespoon grated Parmesan cheese
2 (6-ounce) boneless pork loin chops
1 tablespoon canola oil
1 cup water

Creamed Spinach and Tomatoes
½ cup cherry tomatoes
⅓ cup heavy cream
4 cups baby spinach
⅛ teaspoon salt
⅛ teaspoon ground black pepper

1 Combine salt, pepper, Italian seasoning, flour, and cheese in a small bowl. Coat pork chops in mixture. Set aside.

2 Press the Sauté button on the Instant Pot® and heat oil 30 seconds. Add pork chops to pot and sear 2 minutes on each side. Remove pork from pot and set aside.

3 Pour water into the Instant Pot®. Place pork chops in steamer basket and insert into pot. Lock lid.

4 Press the Manual or Pressure Cook button and adjust cook time to 6 minutes. When timer beeps, quick-release pressure until float valve drops and then unlock lid.

5 Remove steamer basket from pot. Remove pork chops and set aside to allow to rest. Pour out water in pot. Press the Sauté button and add tomatoes. Stir-fry 5 minutes, smooshing tomatoes with the back of a wooden spoon. Add heavy cream, spinach, salt, and pepper. Cook for an additional 2 minutes until spinach is wilted.

6 Transfer mixture to two plates and place pork chops on top. Serve warm.

Simple Barbecue Pork Ribs

Sometimes simple is needed with a hectic schedule. Choose your sauce, buy a rack of ribs, and within the hour, you and your family will be eating barbecue ribs. Don't forget that the Instant Pot® has a timer setting, so the ribs can be ready when you step through your door after a long day.

- **Hands-On Time: 10 minutes**
- **Cook Time: 30 minutes**

Serves 6

1 rack pork ribs (approximately 3½ pounds), cut into 2-rib sections

1½ cups gluten-free barbecue sauce, divided

1 cup water

1 In a medium bowl, toss ribs with ¾ cup barbecue sauce. Refrigerate ribs covered at least 30 minutes or up to overnight.

2 Add water to the Instant Pot® and steamer basket. Arrange ribs standing upright, meaty side facing outward toward the pot walls in basket. Lock lid.

3 Press the Manual or Pressure Cook button and adjust cook time to 30 minutes. When timer beeps, let pressure release naturally until float valve drops and then unlock lid.

4 Transfer ribs to a serving dish and serve warm with remaining barbecue sauce for dipping.

Pork Ragout

Ragout is simply a stew-like dish made with meat or fish and vegetables. But there is nothing simple about this dish. From the succulent pork to the touch of red wine and the fresh veggies, this recipe is excellent straight out of a bowl, served over gluten-free pasta or egg noodles, or with the Basic Polenta recipe found in Chapter 5.

- **Hands-On Time: 15 minutes**
- **Cook Time: 27 minutes**

Serves 6

1 (2-pound) boneless pork butt or shoulder, cut into 2" cubes

2 teaspoons salt

1 teaspoon ground black pepper

1 tablespoon Italian seasoning

1 tablespoon olive oil

1 (15-ounce) can crushed tomatoes, including juice

¼ cup dry red wine

1 small yellow onion, peeled and diced

1 medium carrot, peeled and diced

1 stalk celery, diced

3 cloves garlic, peeled and minced

2 cups chopped chard, ribs removed

4 tablespoons Parmesan cheese

1 Pat pork butt cubes with paper towels. Season with salt, pepper, and Italian seasoning and set aside.

2 Press the Sauté button on the Instant Pot® and heat oil 30 seconds. Add pork to pot and sear 5 minutes, stirring continuously to ensure all sides are seared.

3 Add tomatoes with juice and wine to pot. Scatter onion, carrot, celery, and garlic on top. Lock lid.

4 Press the Manual or Pressure Cook button and adjust cook time to 20 minutes. When timer beeps, let pressure release naturally until float valve drops and then unlock lid. Check pork with two forks to make sure it can easily pull apart. If not, press the Sauté button and simmer unlidded for an additional 10 minutes.

5 Using a fork, shred pork in pot with juices. Add chard and simmer 2 minutes until chard is wilted.

6 Using a slotted spoon, transfer pork ragout to six bowls, garnish with Parmesan cheese, and serve warm.

Hawaiian Pork

This recipe yields succulent pork with a subtle play on sweet and sour. Although a luau is the ideal setting for this meal, there is no need to wrap up the meat in leaves and cook it for 16 hours to enjoy the delicious, mouthwatering flavors and tropical experience. Serve this between a gluten-free bun, in tacos, over rice, or straight out of the pot!

- **Hands-On Time: 10 minutes**
- **Cook Time: 70 minutes**

Serves 8

1 (4-pound) boneless pork butt or shoulder, quartered

2 teaspoons salt

1 teaspoon ground black pepper

2 tablespoons olive oil

2 tablespoons liquid smoke

1 tablespoon smoked paprika

6 cloves garlic, peeled and quartered

1 (20-ounce) can crushed pineapple, including juice

2 teaspoons lime zest

Juice from 1 medium lime

½ teaspoon salt

2 cups beef broth

1 Season all sides of pork with salt and pepper.

2 Press the Sauté button on the Instant Pot® and heat oil 30 seconds. Place pork in pot. Sear meat 5 minutes, making sure to get each side, then remove from pot and set aside.

3 Add liquid smoke, smoked paprika, garlic cloves, crushed pineapple with juice, lime zest, lime juice, and salt to pot. Stir.

4 Add broth and pork to pot. Lock lid.

5 Press the Manual or Pressure Cook button and adjust time to 65 minutes. When timer beeps, let pressure release naturally for 10 minutes. Quick-release any additional pressure until float valve drops and then unlock lid.

6 Using two forks, split pork and incorporate juices. Serve warm.

Herbed Cornmeal Breaded Pork Chops

The herbed and naturally gluten-free cornmeal not only lends a little rustic comfort; it also tricks your brain into thinking the dish has a fried component to it, making it a delicious compromise. You'll be wanting more of these very accessible and mouthwatering pork chops.

- **Hands-On Time: 10 minutes**
- **Cook Time: 15 minutes**

Serves 2

1 large egg
¼ cup cornmeal
1 tablespoon Italian seasoning
1 teaspoon salt
2 (1"-thick) bone-in pork chops
2 tablespoons olive oil
1 cup water

1 In a small bowl, whisk egg. In a second small bowl, combine cornmeal, Italian seasoning, and salt.

2 Dip each pork chop in whisked egg and then dredge in cornmeal mixture. Set aside.

3 Press the Sauté button on the Instant Pot® and heat oil 30 seconds. Place pork chops in pot and brown 5 minutes on each side. Remove chops and set aside.

4 Add water to pot. Insert steamer basket. Place pork chops in basket. Lock lid.

5 Press the Steam button, and adjust the time to 3 minutes. When timer beeps, let pressure release naturally for 5 minutes. Quick-release any additional pressure until float valve drops and then unlock lid.

6 While pressure is releasing, preheat oven to broiler for 500°F.

7 Transfer pork chops to a baking sheet lined with parchment paper. Broil 2 minutes until tops are browned. Remove from heat and serve.

Pork Meatball Bahn Mi

This may seem like a daunting list of ingredients, but you probably have most of them already on hand. And once you take a bite into all of these zesty, fresh flavors, you'll see the reason for so many ingredients: each one balances out the others.

- Hands-On Time: 15 minutes
- Cook Time: 28 minutes

Serves 4

Slaw
1 cup shredded carrots, scrubbed
1 cup julienned radishes
1 cup peeled and finely diced cucumber
¼ cup chopped fresh cilantro
1 tablespoon honey
2 tablespoons rice vinegar
¼ teaspoon salt
2 teaspoons orange zest

Spicy Aioli
½ cup mayonnaise
2 teaspoons sriracha
2 teaspoons freshly squeezed orange juice

Meatballs
1 pound ground pork
2 large eggs
1 teaspoon garlic powder
½ cup old-fashioned oats
2 tablespoons sesame oil, divided
2 cups water

Sandwiches
4 gluten-free baguettes, sliced lengthwise

1 Combine slaw ingredients in a medium bowl. Cover and refrigerate until ready to use.

2 Combine aioli ingredients in a small bowl. Cover and refrigerate until ready to use.

3 In a medium bowl, combine pork, eggs, garlic powder, and oats. Form into twenty meatballs. Set aside.

4 Press the Sauté button on the Instant Pot® and heat 1 tablespoon oil 30 seconds. Place ten meatballs around the edge of pot. Sear meatballs 4 minutes, making sure to get each side. Place meatballs in a 7-cup glass dish and set aside. Add another tablespoon oil and remaining meatballs and sear for 4 minutes. Add meatballs to glass dish.

5 Discard extra juice and oil from the Instant Pot® and add water. Insert steam rack. Place the glass dish on top of the steam rack. Lock lid.

6 Press the Manual or Pressure Cook button and adjust cook time to 20 minutes. When timer beeps, let pressure release naturally for 10 minutes. Quick-release any additional pressure until float valve drops and then unlock lid.

7 Place five meatballs on each sliced baguette. Add slaw. Drizzle with aioli. Serve.

Classic Cuban Picadillo

Serve this meal with rice and black beans to complete the experience of a hearty, happy, and traditional Cuban meal.

- **Hands-On Time: 10 minutes**
- **Cook Time: 18 minutes**

Serves 4

2 tablespoons olive oil

1 medium sweet onion, peeled and diced

1 red bell pepper, seeded and diced

2 small red potatoes, scrubbed and small-diced

1 pound ground beef

1 pound chorizo, ground or cut from casings

3 cloves garlic, peeled and minced

1 teaspoon salt

½ teaspoon ground black pepper

1 tablespoon apple cider vinegar

1 tablespoon cooking sherry

1 (14.5-ounce) can diced fire-roasted tomatoes, including juice

1 (6-ounce) can tomato paste

1 tablespoon capers

1 teaspoon caper juice (from the jar)

⅓ cup pimento-stuffed green olives, sliced

1 tablespoon green olive juice (from the jar)

⅓ cup raisins

1 teaspoon ground cumin

1 teaspoon ground coriander

1 Press the Sauté button on the Instant Pot® and heat oil 30 seconds. Add onion, red bell pepper, and potatoes to pot. Heat 5 minutes until onions are translucent. Add beef and chorizo. Stir-fry 7 minutes until meat is browned. Add garlic and stir 1 minute.

2 Add remaining ingredients to pot. Lock lid.

3 Press the Manual or Pressure Cook button and adjust cook time to 5 minutes. When timer beeps, quick-release pressure until float valve drops and then unlock lid. Stir and serve.

Home-Style Meatloaf

There is a reason meatloaf has been a staple of dinner menus around the country for decades: it is the perfect American comfort food. With just a quick switch to gluten-free bread crumbs or oats, meatloaf can be part of your family table again. Not only is it half of a hearty meat-and-potatoes meal, but it also stirs up happy memories, making it a no-brainer as to why this simple dish has graced many tables over many years.

- **Hands-On Time: 15 minutes**
- **Cook Time: 35 minutes**

Serves 4

Glaze
½ cup ketchup

1 tablespoon dark brown sugar

2 teaspoons Dijon mustard

Meatloaf
1 pound ground beef

1 pound ground pork

3 large eggs

1 cup old-fashioned oats

½ cup peeled and finely diced yellow onion

¼ cup seeded and finely diced red bell pepper

½ cup tomato sauce

2 teaspoons tamari

1 tablespoon Italian seasoning

½ teaspoon smoked paprika

½ teaspoon garlic powder

1 teaspoon salt

½ teaspoon ground black pepper

1 cup water

1 Combine glaze ingredients in a small bowl and set aside.

2 In a large bowl, combine all meatloaf ingredients (except water) with your hands.

3 Form mixture into a ball, flattening the top, then place meatloaf into a 7-cup glass dish. Brush top of meatloaf with ½ of glaze mixture.

4 Add water to the Instant Pot®. Insert steam rack. Place glass dish on top of the steam rack. Lock lid.

5 Press the Meat button and cook for the default time of 35 minutes. When timer beeps, release pressure naturally for 10 minutes. Quick-release any additional pressure until float valve drops and then unlock lid.

6 Remove meatloaf from pot and let cool at room temperature for 10 minutes. Gently tilt glass dish over the sink and pour out any liquid. Brush on remaining glaze. Slice meatloaf and serve warm.

Mexican Flank Steak

Flank steak is often an overlooked cut of beef because of its tough fibers, but you just have to know how to treat it! Marinating before cooking helps tenderize the meat. And once it's cooked, let the steak rest 5 minutes. Once the meat is cool enough to touch, slice it thinly against the grain. This tender flank can go up against any fancy filet mignon.

- **Hands-On Time: 10 minutes**
- **Cook Time: 40 minutes**

Serves 8

¼ cup lime juice

1 tablespoon apple cider vinegar

2 tablespoons honey

1 teaspoon ground cumin

1 teaspoon salt

2 teaspoons sriracha

3 cloves garlic, peeled and minced

½ cup chopped fresh cilantro

3 tablespoons olive oil, divided

2 pounds flank steak, trimmed

1½ cups beef broth

1 In a small bowl, combine lime juice, apple cider vinegar, honey, cumin, salt, sriracha, garlic, cilantro, and 2 tablespoons olive oil. Spread mixture on all sides of steak. Refrigerate steak covered 30 minutes.

2 Press the Sauté button on the Instant Pot® and heat 1 tablespoon oil 30 seconds. Add steak to pot and sear 5 minutes, making sure to brown each side. Add beef broth. Lock lid.

3 Press the Meat button and cook for the default time of 35 minutes. When timer beeps, let pressure release naturally for 5 minutes. Quick-release any additional pressure until float valve drops and then unlock lid.

4 Transfer meat to a cutting board and let rest 5 minutes. Thinly slice beef against the grain and serve.

GIVE YOUR FLANK STEAK SOME KICK WITH JALAPEÑO PESTO

Pulse the following ingredients together for a spicy sauce for your Mexican Flank Steak: 1 tablespoon Dijon mustard, ¼ cup chopped fresh mint, ½ cup chopped fresh parsley, four peeled cloves of garlic, two jalapeños (ends trimmed), 2 teaspoons lemon juice, ¼ cup olive oil. Add the oil slowly until desired consistency. Refrigerate mixture covered until ready to serve.

Loose Beef Barbecue

Savory and tender, Midwest diners have it right when serving this bite of Americana. Similar to a Sloppy Joe, this shredded beef sandwich is packed with flavor and is also easy to prepare. Serve straight out of a bowl, in lettuce wraps, or on gluten-free hamburger buns. Double or triple the recipe during family get-togethers for a crowd-pleasing meal!

- **Hands-On Time: 15 minutes**
- **Cook Time: 65 minutes**

Serves 8

1 cup ketchup

2 tablespoons honey

¼ cup apple cider vinegar

1 tablespoon light brown sugar

1 teaspoon garlic powder

1 teaspoon chili powder

2 tablespoons Dijon mustard

1 (3-pound) boneless chuck roast, quartered

1 teaspoon salt

½ teaspoon ground black pepper

3 tablespoons vegetable oil

1 large yellow onion, peeled and sliced

4 cups beef broth

1 In a small bowl, combine ketchup, honey, apple cider vinegar, brown sugar, garlic powder, chili powder, and Dijon mustard. Refrigerate mixture covered until ready to use.

2 Season roast on all sides with salt and pepper. Press the Sauté button on the Instant Pot® and heat oil 30 seconds. Place meat in pot and sear 5 minutes, making sure to brown each side. Add onion and beef broth. Lock lid.

3 Press the Manual or Pressure Cook button and adjust cook time to 60 minutes. When timer beeps, let pressure release naturally for 5 minutes. Quick-release any additional pressure until float valve drops and then unlock lid. Strain all but ¼ cup of liquid from pot. Set strained liquid aside.

4 Using two forks, shred meat. Add ketchup mixture to pot. Continue to use the forks to shred meat and stir in ketchup mixture to moisten the meat. If more liquid is needed, use set-aside strained liquid.

5 Using a slotted spoon, transfer meat to eight bowls, gluten-free buns, or lettuce wraps, and serve warm.

Chi-Town Italian Beef and Peppers

You don't have to travel to Chicago to enjoy one of the city's original recipes with thin slices of beef, slivered peppers, and chopped pickled veggies known as *giardiniera*. The bread of this sandwich is usually "wet," meaning that it has been dipped in au jus, or "gravy," as the locals call it, which is the liquid that the meat and peppers were cooked in.

- **Hands-On Time: 15 minutes**
- **Cook Time: 65 minutes**

Serves 8

¼ cup olive oil

1 tablespoon Italian seasoning

1 teaspoon garlic powder

1 teaspoon smoked paprika

½ teaspoon red pepper flakes

1 teaspoon salt

½ teaspoon ground black pepper

1 green bell pepper, seeded and sliced

1 red bell pepper, seeded and sliced

1 yellow bell pepper, seeded and sliced

1 large yellow onion, peeled and sliced

1 (3-pound) boneless chuck roast, quartered

4 cups beef broth

1 cup chopped jarred giardiniera, drained

1 In a large bowl, combine oil, Italian seasoning, garlic powder, smoked paprika, red pepper flakes, salt, and black pepper. Add sliced bell peppers, onion, and quartered roast and toss. Refrigerate roast covered at least 30 minutes or up to overnight.

2 Press the Sauté button on the Instant Pot® and add in meat, veggies, and marinade. Sear meat 5 minutes, making sure to brown each side. Add beef broth. Lock lid.

3 Press the Manual or Pressure Cook button and adjust cook time to 60 minutes. When timer beeps, let pressure release naturally for 5 minutes. Quick-release any additional pressure until float valve drops and then unlock lid. Strain all but ¼ cup of liquid from pot. Set strained liquid aside.

4 Transfer meat to a cutting board. Let meat rest 5 minutes, then thinly slice and add back to pot with veggies and liquid to moisten meat.

5 Using a slotted spoon, transfer meat and veggies to eight bowls, gluten-free buns, or lettuce wraps. Garnish with giardiniera and serve.

Easy Beef Biryani

Biryani, traditionally an Indian and Pakistani dish, is typically made with chicken or lamb. The spices actually work beautifully with beef. By the way, the premium varieties of this dish include a little saffron, so if you have some in the pantry, throw in ⅛ teaspoon.

- **Hands-On Time: 10 minutes**
- **Cook Time: 25 minutes**

Serves 6

1 tablespoon ghee or unsalted butter

1 medium yellow onion, peeled and sliced

1 pound top round, cut into ½" strips

¼ cup golden raisins

1 tablespoon minced fresh ginger

2 cloves garlic, peeled and minced

½ teaspoon ground cloves

½ teaspoon ground cardamom

½ teaspoon ground coriander

½ teaspoon ground black pepper

½ teaspoon cinnamon

½ teaspoon ground cumin

1 teaspoon salt

1 cup plain full-fat yogurt

1 (28-ounce) can whole stewed tomatoes, including juice

2 cups cooked basmati rice

¼ cup chopped fresh mint leaves

1 Press the Sauté button on the Instant Pot® and heat ghee 30 seconds. Add onion to pot and sauté 5 minutes until onions are browned and starting to caramelize. Add all remaining ingredients except rice and mint to pot. Lock lid.

2 Press the Manual or Pressure Cook button and adjust cook time to 10 minutes. When timer beeps, quick-release pressure until float valve drops and then unlock lid. Simmer mixture uncovered for 10 minutes until most of liquid has evaporated.

3 Transfer into six bowls over cooked basmati rice. Garnish with mint leaves and serve warm.

Beef Burgundy in a Pinch

Chef Julia Child is known for her classic Boeuf Bourguignon, but don't we all think that she would have cut some corners if she'd had an Instant Pot®? Well, maybe not, but the rest of us could use a piece of her mastery without the hours of time and years of practice, and this recipe fits that bill! Serve this over egg noodles or rice to complete the dish.

- **Hands-On Time: 15 minutes**
- **Cook Time: 27 minutes**

Serves 4

2 tablespoons gluten-free all-purpose flour

1 teaspoon salt

1 teaspoon ground black pepper

2 pounds boneless beef-round steak, cut into 1" pieces

4 tablespoons olive oil, divided

3 shallots, peeled and diced

3 cloves garlic, peeled and minced

1 cup dry red wine

2 cups sliced white mushrooms

2 medium carrots, peeled and thinly sliced

2 tablespoons fresh thyme leaves

1 cup beef broth

2 tablespoons tomato paste

¼ cup chopped fresh parsley

1 In a small bowl, combine flour, salt, and pepper. Dredge steak pieces in mixture until well coated.

2 Press the Sauté button on the Instant Pot® and heat 2 tablespoons of oil 30 seconds. Add half of steak to pot. Sear 4 minutes, browning all sides of steak. Transfer to a plate. Heat remaining oil and sear remaining steak 4 minutes. Transfer steak to plate. Add shallots and garlic to pot. Stir-fry 2 minutes.

3 Deglaze pot by adding red wine, scraping any bits from the bottom or sides of pot. Cook for an additional 2 minutes to allow alcohol to cook off.

4 Add mushrooms, carrots, thyme, beef broth, and tomato paste to pot. Lock lid.

5 Press the Manual or Pressure Cook button and adjust cook time to 15 minutes. When timer beeps, let pressure release naturally until float valve drops and then unlock lid.

6 Transfer mixture to a serving dish and garnish with parsley. Serve warm.

Simply Cheesy Meatballs

Whether you put these meatballs on some pasta or spiralized veggies, slap them on a gluten-free bun with some melted mozzarella, or just want to eat them out of the bowl, these juicy—not to mention gluten-free—meatballs will have you coming back for more and more!

- **Hands-On Time: 15 minutes**
- **Cook Time: 30 minutes**

Serves 4

½ pound ground beef

½ pound ground pork

2 large eggs

1 tablespoon Italian seasoning

¼ cup grated Parmesan cheese

¼ cup ricotta cheese

½ cup gluten-free bread crumbs

3 tablespoons olive oil, divided

2 cups marinara sauce

2 cups water

WHAT CAN I SUBSTITUTE FOR GLUTEN-FREE BREAD CRUMBS?

Although there are gluten-free bread crumbs available on the market, there are several things you can do in a pinch. Using a small food processor, simply pulse gluten-free toast, gluten-free cereal, or even corn tortillas (which are exceptional on a fresh piece of cod!).

1 In a medium bowl, combine beef, pork, eggs, Italian seasoning, Parmesan cheese, ricotta cheese, and bread crumbs. Form mixture into twenty meatballs. Set aside.

2 Press the Sauté button on the Instant Pot® and heat 2 tablespoons oil 30 seconds. Place ten meatballs around the edge of pot. Sear meatballs 5 minutes, making sure to get each side. Set aside. Add 1 table-spoon oil to pot and sear remaining meat-balls 5 minutes.

3 Transfer seared meatballs to a 7-cup glass dish. Top with sauce.

4 Discard extra juice and oil from the Instant Pot® and add water. Insert steam rack. Place the glass dish on top of the steam rack. Lock lid.

5 Press the Manual or Pressure Cook button and adjust cook time to 20 minutes. When timer beeps, let pressure release naturally for 10 minutes. Quick-release any additional pressure until float valve drops and then unlock lid.

6 Transfer meatballs to a serving dish and serve warm.

Porcupine Meatballs

If you remember the days when pet rocks were king and disco was cool, then you probably remember eating porcupine meatballs. If you are not from this bygone era, then enjoy the treat of many who came before you. The rice sticking out of the meatballs creates a porcupine effect, making them more fun to eat!

- **Hands-On Time: 15 minutes**
- **Cook Time: 23 minutes**

Serves 4

1 pound ground beef

½ cup white rice

1 large egg

2 tablespoons peeled and finely diced yellow onion

1 teaspoon salt

½ teaspoon ground black pepper

½ teaspoon garlic powder

3 tablespoons olive oil, divided

1 (10.75-ounce) can condensed cream of tomato soup

¼ cup water

1 tablespoon light brown sugar

2 teaspoons Worcestershire sauce

½ cup chopped fresh parsley

1 In a medium bowl, combine beef, rice, egg, onion, salt, pepper, and garlic powder. Form mixture into twenty meatballs. Set aside.

2 Press the Sauté button on the Instant Pot® and heat 2 tablespoons oil 30 seconds. Place ten meatballs around the edge of pot. Sear meatballs 4 minutes, making sure to get each side. Set aside. Add 1 tablespoon oil to pot and sear remaining meatballs 4 minutes. Add first batch of meatballs to pot.

3 In a small bowl, whisk together tomato soup, water, brown sugar, and Worcestershire sauce. Pour mixture over meatballs.

4 Press the Manual or Pressure Cook button and adjust cook time to 15 minutes. When timer beeps, let pressure release naturally for 10 minutes. Quick-release any additional pressure until float valve drops and then unlock lid.

5 Transfer meatballs and sauce to a serving dish and garnish with fresh parsley. Serve warm.

Quick Beef and Broccoli

If you miss ordering Beef and Broccoli from the takeout menu, but don't miss the hidden gluten, make your own using tamari and fresh ingredients. Serve this healthy, gluten-free version in a takeout box with chopsticks for the full experience. You can pick up these boxes at craft stores or buy them online.

- **Hands-On Time: 10 minutes**
- **Cook Time: 4 minutes**

Serves 2

Sauce
2 cloves garlic, peeled and minced
⅓ cup tamari
¼ cup rice wine vinegar
2 tablespoons honey
1 tablespoon sesame oil
¼ teaspoon ground ginger
¼ teaspoon salt
⅛ teaspoon cayenne pepper

Beef and Broccoli
1 medium head broccoli, chopped
1 (1-pound) boneless sirloin, trimmed and sliced into 3" strips
1 cup water

1 In a medium bowl, combine sauce ingredients. Set aside 2 tablespoons of sauce. Add beef to the bowl and toss. Refrigerate beef for 30 minutes.

2 Press the Sauté button on the Instant Pot® and let heat up 2 minutes. Place meat in pot and stir-fry 2 minutes. Add broccoli and toss 1 minute. Transfer beef and broccoli to a large bowl.

3 Pour water into the Instant Pot®. Insert steamer basket. Add beef and broccoli to basket. Lock lid.

4 Press the Manual or Pressure Cook button and adjust cook time to 1 minute. When timer beeps, quick-release pressure until float valve drops and then unlock lid.

5 Transfer beef and broccoli to a serving dish and toss with remaining sauce. Serve warm.

Meatballs with Asian Sauce

An Asian twist on the Italian meatball, these sweet, sour, and spicy flavors work in conjunction with the juicy beef and pork to make this recipe a hit. Serve with rice for dinner, and then on a gluten-free roll with a simple slaw the next day for lunch!

- **Hands-On Time: 15 minutes**
- **Cook Time: 28 minutes**

Serves 4

Sauce
¼ cup tamari
¼ cup honey
⅛ cup rice vinegar
1 teaspoon sriracha
1" knob ginger, peeled and sliced
2 teaspoons sesame oil

Meatballs
½ pound ground beef
½ pound ground pork
1 large egg
1 medium shallot, peeled and finely diced
1 tablespoon Chinese five-spice powder
3 tablespoons sesame oil, divided
2 cups water

1 In a small bowl, combine sauce ingredients. Set aside.

2 In a medium bowl, combine beef, pork, egg, shallot, and Chinese five-spice powder. Form mixture into twenty meatballs. Set aside.

3 Press the Sauté button on the Instant Pot® and warm 2 tablespoons oil 30 seconds. Place ten meatballs around the edge of pot. Sear meatballs 4 minutes, making sure to get each side. Set aside. Add 1 table-spoon oil to pot and sear remaining meat-balls 4 minutes.

4 Transfer seared meatballs to a 7-cup glass dish. Top with sauce.

5 Discard extra juice and oil from the Instant Pot®. Add water to pot. Insert steam rack. Place the glass dish on top of the steam rack. Lock lid.

6 Press the Manual or Pressure Cook button and adjust cook time to 20 minutes. When timer beeps, let pressure release naturally for 10 minutes. Quick-release any additional pressure until float valve drops and then unlock lid.

7 Transfer meatballs to a serving dish and serve warm.

Lamb Keftedes

Keftedes are simply Greek meatballs. The cinnamon and garlic powder, along with the fresh herbs, combine beautifully with the earthiness of the ground lamb. Although they are so tasty right out of the pot, you can also serve them with tzatziki, either as a dipping sauce or as a condiment on a gluten-free pita pocket with fresh diced tomatoes.

- **Hands-On Time: 15 minutes**
- **Cook Time: 18 minutes**

Serves 4

1 pound ground lamb

2 large eggs

1 tablespoon peeled and finely diced cucumber

1 large carrot, scrubbed and grated

1 tablespoon chopped fresh mint leaves

1 tablespoon chopped fresh dill

1 teaspoon garlic powder

⅛ teaspoon ground cinnamon

1 tablespoon lemon zest

½ cup old-fashioned oats

3 tablespoons olive oil, divided

2 cups water

MAKE A QUICK TZATZIKI SAUCE

In a medium bowl, combine the following ingredients: 1 cup plain full-fat Greek yogurt, 1 cup peeled and diced English cucumber, 1 tablespoon chopped fresh dill, 1 tablespoon minced fresh garlic, 2 tablespoons lemon juice, 2 teaspoons lemon zest, ½ teaspoon salt, ½ teaspoon ground black pepper. Refrigerate covered until ready to use.

1 In a medium bowl, combine lamb, eggs, cucumber, carrot, mint, dill, garlic powder, cinnamon, lemon zest, and oats. Form mixture into twenty meatballs. Set aside.

2 Press the Sauté button on the Instant Pot® and heat 2 tablespoons oil 30 seconds. Place ten meatballs around the edge of pot. Sear meatballs 4 minutes, making sure to get each side. Set aside. Add 1 tablespoon oil to pot and sear remaining meatballs 4 minutes.

3 Transfer seared meatballs to a 7-cup glass dish.

4 Discard extra juice and oil from the Instant Pot®. Add water to pot. Insert steam rack. Place the glass dish on top of the steam rack. Lock lid.

5 Press the Manual or Pressure Cook button and adjust cook time to 10 minutes. When timer beeps, let pressure release naturally for 10 minutes. Quick-release any additional pressure until float valve drops and then unlock lid.

6 Transfer meatballs to a serving dish and serve warm.

Seafood and Fish Main Dishes

Seafood is one of those meals that is often ordered at restaurants but overlooked at home. A lot of home chefs are timid when it comes to cooking fish and shellfish, but that's a shame because it is a naturally gluten-free food that is low in calories and high in nutrition. Fish and shellfish are also some of the quickest meals you can cook in your Instant Pot®. In addition, the steaming functionality of the appliance makes for tender and moist meals.

The Instant Pot® easily and perfectly cooks your seafood with its steam and pressure capabilities. The recipes in this chapter call for short cooking times and quick pressure releases. You don't want to do a natural pressure release with most fish, as it will continue to cook if the pressure releases slowly. From Coconut Poached Halibut to Summer Salmon Salad, this chapter covers a variety of delicious gluten-free recipes and types of fish that will have you eating seafood on a regular basis.

Seasoned Steamed Shrimp

Steamed shrimp make for such a decadent, low-calorie, and flavor-filled dinner option—and they are even easy to cook. Ready in a snap, these pink crustaceans can be served with a little melted butter or cocktail sauce. For a complete gluten-free meal, place some asparagus spears over the shrimp before cooking.

- **Hands-On Time: 5 minutes**
- **Cook Time: 0 minutes**

Serves 4

2 pounds large uncooked shrimp, peeled and deveined

1 lemon, quartered

2 tablespoons Old Bay Seasoning

1 cup water

WHY SHOULD I STEAM SHRIMP WITH SQUEEZED LEMONS?

The reason this recipe calls for the lemons in the pot even though the juice has already been squeezed is because there are bright oils in the rind that add another level of acidic flavor to the shrimp. The same is true for limes and oranges, which also pair well with shrimp if you are looking for a change of pace.

1 Place shrimp in a bowl. Squeeze lemon quarters over shrimp. Toss squeezed lemons in bowl with shrimp. Sprinkle Old Bay Seasoning over shrimp and toss until evenly coated.

2 Add water to the Instant Pot® and insert steamer basket. Place shrimp in basket. Lock lid.

3 Press the Steam button and adjust time to 0 minutes. When timer beeps, quick-release pressure until float valve drops and then unlock lid. Discard lemons.

4 Transfer shrimp to serving dish and serve warm or cold.

Almond-Crusted Cod

Cod is a firm yet flaky whitefish that stands up well to steaming. Moist and delicious, with a little crunch on top, this dish is simple to cook yet complex in its textures. Even folks who are wary of fish will be won over by this yummy, non-fishy fish recipe.

- **Hands-On Time: 5 minutes**
- **Cook Time: 7 minutes**

Serves 2

1 tablespoon Dijon mustard
1 teaspoon fresh lemon juice
2 tablespoons cornmeal
¼ cup chopped unsalted almonds
½ teaspoon salt
2 (5-ounce) cod fillets
1 cup water

1 Preheat oven to broiler for 500°F.

2 In a small bowl, combine mustard, lemon juice, cornmeal, almonds, and salt to form a thick paste.

3 Pat cod fillets dry with a paper towel. Rub paste on the top of each fillet.

4 Add water to the Instant Pot®. Place fillets in steamer basket and insert into pot. Lock lid.

5 Press the Manual or Pressure Cook button and adjust cook time to 5 minutes. When timer beeps, quick-release pressure until float valve drops and then unlock lid.

6 Transfer fillets to a baking sheet lined with parchment paper. Broil fillets at 500°F for 2 minutes until tops are browned.

7 Remove fillets from oven and serve warm.

Butter Cod

A great source of healthy omega-3 fatty acids, cod is a flaky whitefish that takes on the flavors it is cooked with. In this case, the salty little capers and the creamy butter work as an ideal pairing of flavors for this simple fish. The non-fishy taste of this fish makes it popular with children and picky eaters.

- **Hands-On Time: 5 minutes**
- **Cook Time: 7 minutes**

Serves 4

4 (5-ounce) cod fillets
1 teaspoon salt
½ teaspoon ground black
  pepper
1 cup water
4 tablespoons unsalted
  butter, divided into 8 pats
4 teaspoons capers, drained

1 Preheat oven to broiler for 500°F.

2 Pat cod fillets dry with a paper towel. Season with salt and pepper.

3 Add water to the Instant Pot®. Place fillets in steamer basket and insert into pot. Lock lid.

4 Press the Manual or Pressure Cook button and adjust cook time to 5 minutes. When timer beeps, quick-release pressure until float valve drops and then unlock lid.

5 Transfer fillets to a baking sheet lined with parchment paper. Add two pats butter to each fillet. Broil fillets 2 minutes until tops are browned.

6 Transfer fish to four plates, garnish with capers, and serve warm.

Monkfish with Lemon-Caper Butter Sauce

There is no need for a long list of ingredients when making monkfish. Just let its rich, buttery flavor shine with a few simple seasoning choices. Known as the poor man's lobster, this little gem of a fish, although terribly unattractive, will have you feeling like a royal. Cod can be substituted in this recipe if monkfish is not available.

- **Hands-On Time: 5 minutes**
- **Cook Time: 6 minutes**

Serves 2

2 (6-ounce, 1"-thick) monkfish fillets

2 tablespoons fresh lemon juice

2 tablespoons capers

1 teaspoon salt

1 teaspoon lemon zest

2 tablespoons unsalted butter, cut into 4 pats

1 cup water

1 tablespoon chopped fresh parsley

1 Place a piece of aluminum foil in the steamer basket. Place fillets on foil. Create a "boat" with the foil by bringing up the edges about 2".

2 Pour lemon juice on fish. Add capers to fish. Season fish with salt and lemon zest. Add two pats butter to each fillet.

3 Add water to the Instant Pot®. Insert steam rack into the Instant Pot®, place fillets in the steamer basket, and place the steamer basket on the steam rack. Lock lid.

4 Press the Manual or Pressure Cook button and adjust cook time to 6 minutes. Quick-release pressure until float valve drops and then unlock lid.

5 Transfer fish to two plates. Garnish each fillet with chopped parsley and serve warm.

Coconut Poached Halibut

Like cod, halibut is a flaky whitefish that takes on the flavors it is cooked with. Poaching the fish fillets in coconut milk and curry paste makes this dish fancy and a bit exotic—not to mention easy to make. The simple spices and coconut milk also provide a tasty Thai-inspired broth.

- **Hands-On Time: 5 minutes**
- **Cook Time: 3 minutes**

Serves 2

1 (13.5-ounce) can coconut milk
Juice of 1 lime
Zest of 1 lime
2 teaspoons red curry paste
2 teaspoons honey
⅛ teaspoon red pepper flakes
1 pound halibut fillets, cubed
½ cup julienned fresh basil leaves, divided

1 Whisk together milk, lime juice, lime zest, red curry paste, honey, and pepper flakes in the Instant Pot®. Add halibut and ¼ cup basil. Lock lid.

2 Press the Manual or Pressure Cook button and adjust cook time to 3 minutes. When timer beeps, quick-release pressure until float valve drops and then unlock lid.

3 Ladle mixture into two bowls and garnish with remaining basil. Serve warm.

Sea Bass with Peach Salsa

Similar to halibut, sea bass is firm and meaty, yet flaky and mild at the same time. And, it is not even a bass: it is actually a Patagonian toothfish. It was named *sea bass* to make it more appealing and easier to sell to a mass market. In this recipe, the simple buttery nature of this fish pairs nicely with the sweet and fresh flavors of the homemade peach salsa.

- **Hands-On Time: 5 minutes**
- **Cook Time: 3 minutes**

Serves 2

Peach Salsa
1 cup peeled and diced peaches
1 Roma tomato, seeded and diced
½ cup peeled and diced cucumbers
¼ cup chopped fresh parsley
1 shallot, peeled and minced
1 tablespoon lime juice
2 tablespoons olive oil
½ teaspoon salt

Fish
2 (5-ounce) sea bass fillets
1 teaspoon salt
½ teaspoon ground black pepper
1 cup water

1 In a small bowl, combine salsa ingredients and refrigerate covered until ready to use.

2 Season fillets with salt and pepper.

3 Add water to the Instant Pot®. Place sea bass in steamer basket and insert basket into pot. Lock lid.

4 Press the Manual or Pressure Cook button and adjust cook time to 3 minutes. When timer beeps, quick-release pressure until float valve drops and then unlock lid.

5 Transfer fish and toppings to two plates. Garnish with salsa and serve warm.

Fish Taco Lettuce Wraps

Full of flavor and the added texture of crunchy slaw, these wraps are perfect on a summer evening while drinking a gluten-free beer surrounded by your friends. Serve soft tortillas next to the lettuce wraps for your gluten-loving guests: the fillings are the stars of this meal!

- **Hands-On Time: 15 minutes**
- **Cook Time: 3 minutes**

Serves 8

Sauce
1 cup mayonnaise
1 tablespoon capers
Juice of ½ lime
⅛ teaspoon hot sauce

Slaw
½ cup grated cabbage
1 large carrot, peeled and grated
2 small radishes, peeled and julienned
Juice of ½ lime
1 tablespoon olive oil
⅛ teaspoon hot sauce
¼ cup chopped fresh cilantro
½ teaspoon salt

Fish
1 pound cod, cubed
3 tablespoons lime juice
1 teaspoon garlic salt
¼ teaspoon cayenne pepper
1 tablespoon olive oil
1 cup water

Extras
1 avocado, peeled, pitted, and diced
½ cup diced tomatoes, seasoned with ⅛ teaspoon salt
10 large lettuce leaves

1 Blend sauce ingredients until smooth. Refrigerate covered at least 30 minutes or up to overnight.

2 In a medium bowl, combine slaw ingredients. Refrigerate covered at least 30 minutes or up to overnight.

3 In a large bowl, combine fish, lime juice, garlic salt, cayenne pepper, and olive oil, and refrigerate covered for 15 minutes.

4 Add water to the Instant Pot®. Insert steam rack. Place steamer basket on top of steam rack. Place cod in an even row in steamer basket. Pour in additional marinade from large bowl for steaming aromatics. Lock lid.

5 Press the Manual or Pressure Cook button and adjust cook time to 3 minutes. When timer beeps, quick-release pressure until float valve drops and then unlock lid.

6 Transfer fish to a serving bowl. Assemble fish taco wraps by adding equal amounts fish, slaw, avocado, and tomatoes to each lettuce leaf. Drizzle with sauce.

Crab-Stuffed Sole Roulade

Sole is a long, thin fillet, so it can be rolled up to fit easily in the Instant Pot®. Try adding vegetables, pesto, or simply butter and herbs for an equally delicious twist. Snapper and tilapia can also be rolled and stuffed this way.

- **Hands-On Time: 5 minutes**
- **Cook Time: 3 minutes**

Serves 4

1 cup lump crabmeat, picked over for shells
4 teaspoons mayonnaise
1 teaspoon prepared horseradish
1 teaspoon lemon juice
1 teaspoon chopped fresh dill
4 (5-ounce) sole fillets
1 teaspoon salt
½ teaspoon ground black pepper
1 cup water
4 tablespoons gluten-free bread crumbs
2 tablespoons unsalted butter, melted

1 Lightly grease a 7-cup glass dish with either oil or cooking spray.

2 In a medium bowl, combine crab, mayonnaise, horseradish, lemon juice, and chopped dill. Set aside.

3 Season fillets with salt and pepper. Spread ¼ crab mixture on the darker side of each fillet. Roll up fillets and place seam-side down in greased glass dish.

4 Add water to the Instant Pot®. Insert steam rack and place glass dish on steam rack. Lock lid.

5 Press the Manual or Pressure Cook button and adjust cook time to 1 minute. When timer beeps, quick-release pressure until float valve drops and then unlock lid.

6 Preheat oven to broiler for 500°F.

7 In a small bowl, combine bread crumbs and butter. Evenly distribute mixture to tops of each rolled fillet.

8 Transfer dish with fillets to oven. Broil 2 minutes until browned. Serve warm.

Salmon with Citrus Horseradish-Mustard Aioli

There are many bold flavors in this recipe, and they come together in harmony to create an explosion of taste. Start with fresh salmon fillets and let the Instant Pot® work its magic while you prepare the aioli. If you want a special kick, buy a knob of fresh horseradish and peel and grate it in, subbing out the prepared horseradish!

- **Hands-On Time: 5 minutes**
- **Cook Time: 5 minutes**

Serves 2

Aioli
¼ cup mayonnaise
1 tablespoon lemon juice
1 teaspoon lemon zest
2 teaspoons Dijon mustard
2 teaspoons prepared horseradish
1 clove garlic, peeled and minced

Salmon
2 (5-ounce) salmon fillets
½ teaspoon salt
1 cup water
1 tablespoon chopped fresh dill

1 In a small bowl, combine aioli ingredients. Refrigerate covered until ready to serve.

2 Pat salmon fillets dry with a paper towel and place in steamer basket. Season fillets with salt.

3 Add water to the Instant Pot®. Insert steam rack. Place steamer basket on top of steam rack. Lock lid.

4 Press the Manual or Pressure Cook button and adjust cook time to 5 minutes. When timer beeps, quick-release pressure until float valve drops and then unlock lid.

5 Transfer fish to two plates and drizzle sauce over each fillet. Garnish with dill and serve immediately.

Catfish Bites with Creamy Slaw

Y'all, it doesn't get more down South than catfish and slaw. The only difference with this recipe is that the catfish isn't deep-fried, so your scale will appreciate the effort! Try making the slaw the night before, as the flavors will come together overnight. Who knew that a good ol' Southern meal could be gluten-free *and* tasty?!

- **Hands-On Time: 5 minutes**
- **Cook Time: 3 minutes**

Serves 4

Creamy Slaw

1 (14-ounce) bag coleslaw mix (shredded cabbage and carrots)

½ cup mayonnaise

⅓ cup sour cream

2 teaspoons granulated sugar

2 teaspoons dill pickle juice, from the jar

2 teaspoons Dijon mustard

½ teaspoon salt

¼ teaspoon ground black pepper

Catfish

1 cup water

2 pounds catfish fillets, rinsed and cut into 1" pieces

1 teaspoon salt

¼ teaspoon ground black pepper

1 In a small bowl, combine slaw ingredients and refrigerate covered until ready to serve.

2 Add water to the Instant Pot®. Season catfish with salt and pepper. Place fish in steamer basket and insert into pot. Lock lid.

3 Press the Manual or Pressure Cook button and adjust cook time to 3 minutes. When timer beeps, quick-release pressure until float valve drops and then unlock lid.

4 Transfer catfish to four plates. Serve warm with chilled slaw.

Ginger-Glazed Mahi-Mahi

The Japanese knew what they were doing when they served ginger with sushi, as there is just something magical about the flavor combination of ginger and fish. The other spices in this dish further elevate this magic. The simplicity of this recipe makes it easy to whip up when you have little time to spare. Serve with vegetables, rice, or mixed greens!

- **Hands-On Time: 5 minutes**
- **Cook Time: 5 minutes**

Serves 2

2 tablespoons tamari

2 tablespoons rice wine vinegar

2 teaspoons sesame oil

2 tablespoons honey

1 teaspoon peeled and grated ginger

⅛ teaspoon cayenne pepper

2 (6-ounce) mahi-mahi fillets, 1" thick

1 cup water

1 Whisk together tamari, rice wine vinegar, sesame oil, honey, ginger, and cayenne pepper. Brush half of glaze on mahi-mahi fillets.

2 Add water to the Instant Pot®. Insert steamer basket. Add fillets to basket. Lock lid.

3 Press the Manual or Pressure Cook button and adjust cook time to 5 minutes. When timer beeps, let pressure release naturally for 5 minutes. Quick-release any additional pressure until float valve drops and then unlock lid.

4 Transfer fish to two plates and brush with remaining glaze. Serve warm.

Summer Salmon Salad

Fresh and full of superfoods, this salad will boost your immune system—but all you will know is that your taste buds are dancing in delight. For less of a kick in the dressing, substitute yellow mustard for Dijon. For a heartier kick, sub with horseradish mustard. The varieties of mustard are so plentiful that you can enjoy a different salad each time. This meal is also great with cod, shrimp, or even lobster!

- **Hands-On Time: 5 minutes**
- **Cook Time: 5 minutes**

Serves 2

Dressing

¼ cup honey
¼ cup Dijon mustard
¼ cup apple cider vinegar
2 tablespoons olive oil
1 clove garlic, peeled and
   minced

Salmon

2 (5-ounce) salmon fillets
½ teaspoon salt
1 cup water

Salad

4 cups arugula
1 Roma tomato, diced
¼ cup fresh blueberries
4 tablespoons peeled and
   diced red onion
4 tablespoons crumbled feta
   cheese
2 tablespoons chopped
   pecans
2 tablespoons salted
   sunflower seeds

1. In a small bowl, whisk together dressing ingredients. Refrigerate covered until ready to serve.

2. Pat salmon fillets dry with a paper towel and place in steamer basket. Season fillets with salt.

3. Add water to the Instant Pot®. Insert steam rack. Place steamer basket on steam rack. Lock lid.

4. Press the Manual or Pressure Cook button and adjust cook time to 5 minutes. When timer beeps, quick-release pressure until float valve drops and then unlock lid.

5. While salmon is cooking, prepare two salads by dividing salad ingredients between two bowls. Toss with dressing. Place cooked salmon fillets on top of each salad and serve.

Steamed Mussels with Tomato-Garlic Sauce

Fairly inexpensive and very tasty, mussels are a great seafood to put in your rotation of meals. They are also a hands-on and festive dish to serve to get a group of friends or family members smiling and talking. To dress up this dish, serve over gluten-free linguini and add a piece of gluten-free toasted bread on the side. Fast and scrumptious!

- **Hands-On Time: 10 minutes**
- **Cook Time: 8 minutes**

Serves 4

2 tablespoons unsalted butter

1 medium yellow onion, peeled and diced

4 cloves garlic, peeled and minced

1 cup dry white wine

1 (14.5-ounce) can diced tomatoes, including juice

1 teaspoon salt

1 teaspoon smoked paprika

Juice of 1 lemon

2 pounds fresh mussels, cleaned and debearded

¼ cup chopped fresh basil leaves

1 Press the Sauté button on the Instant Pot®. Add butter to pot and heat 30 seconds. Add onion and sauté 5 minutes until translucent. Add garlic and cook for an additional minute. Stir in white wine and cook 2 minutes.

2 Add tomatoes with juice, salt, smoked paprika, and lemon juice. Insert steamer basket. Place mussels in basket. Lock lid.

3 Press the Manual or Pressure Cook button and adjust cook time to 0 minutes. When timer beeps, quick-release pressure until float valve drops and then unlock lid.

4 Remove mussels and discard any that haven't opened. Transfer mussels to four bowls and distribute liquid from pot equally among bowls. Garnish with basil. Serve immediately.

CAN FOOD COOK IN 0 MINUTES?
If you are confused about how some recipes require 0 minutes to cook, it's not a typo. Some veggies and seafoods that only require minimal steaming are set at zero cooking time, which is the time that it takes the Instant Pot® to achieve pressure.

Blue Cheese Pancetta Mussels

This is just a bowl of good ol' bar food at the beach. Mussels are an underused bivalve, and it's a shame. They are easy to make and very inexpensive, making them a perfect choice for a party and impressing your guests with a food that most people don't choose to cook on a regular basis, if at all. You can also use water or broth in lieu of the gluten-free beer.

- **Hands-On Time: 10 minutes**
- **Cook Time: 8 minutes**

Serves 4

2 tablespoons unsalted butter

4 ounces pancetta or thick-sliced bacon, diced

1 medium red onion, peeled and diced

4 cloves garlic, peeled and minced

2 cans gluten-free beer

2 pounds fresh mussels, cleaned and debearded

1 teaspoon salt

1 teaspoon smoked paprika

½ cup crumbled blue cheese

¼ cup chopped fresh basil leaves

1 Press the Sauté button on the Instant Pot®. Add butter to pot and heat 30 seconds. Add pancetta and onion and cook 5 minutes until onions are translucent. Add garlic and cook for an additional minute. Stir in beer and cook 2 minutes.

2 Insert steamer basket into pot. Place mussels in basket. Sprinkle mussels with salt and smoked paprika. Lock lid.

3 Press the Manual or Pressure Cook button and adjust cook time to 0 minutes. When timer beeps, quick-release pressure until float valve drops and then unlock lid.

4 Remove mussels and discard any that haven't opened. Transfer mussels to four bowls and distribute liquid, veggies, and pancetta from pot equally among bowls. Garnish each bowl with blue cheese and basil. Serve immediately.

New England Lobster Rolls

This classic to New Englanders can be yours in minutes. The lobster meat shines with very few seasonings. Traditionally served on a top-split buttered hot dog bun, the lobster is great on its own, in a lettuce wrap, or on whatever gluten-free bread you enjoy!

- **Hands-On Time: 2 minutes**
- **Cook Time: 6 minutes**

Serves 4

1 cup water

1 tablespoon Old Bay Seasoning

4 (6-ounce) uncooked lobster tails, thawed

¼ cup mayonnaise

1 stalk celery, diced

1 tablespoon lemon juice

1 teaspoon lemon zest

½ teaspoon smoked paprika

½ teaspoon salt

¼ teaspoon ground black pepper

¼ cup unsalted butter, melted

4 gluten-free top-split buns

1 cup shredded lettuce

1 Add water and Old Bay Seasoning to the Instant Pot® and insert steamer basket. Add lobster tails to basket. Lock lid.

2 Press the Steam button and adjust time to 4 minutes. When timer beeps, quick-release pressure until float valve drops and then unlock lid. Transfer tails to an ice bath to stop the lobster from overcooking.

3 Remove lobster meat from shells. Roughly chop meat and transfer to a medium bowl. Combine lobster with mayonnaise, celery, lemon juice, lemon zest, smoked paprika, salt, and pepper.

4 Brush butter on each side of buns. Brown buns in a skillet over medium heat 2 minutes. Distribute lobster and lettuce among buns and serve.

Crawfish Étouffée

Although similar to gumbo, étouffée is thicker and usually includes only one protein instead of the mix of proteins found in gumbo. Just like all good Louisiana cooking, this dish starts out with what is known as the Cajun holy trinity: onion, celery, and green pepper. Starting out with these three ingredients will ensure you are on the way to impressing Emeril Lagasse with your Louisiana cooking skills...BAM!

- **Hands-On Time: 15 minutes**
- **Cook Time: 15 minutes**

Serves 4

6 tablespoons unsalted butter

¼ cup gluten-free all-purpose flour

1 medium sweet onion, peeled and diced

2 stalks celery, diced

1 medium green bell pepper, seeded and diced

4 cloves garlic, peeled and minced

1 (14.5-ounce) can diced tomatoes, including juice

¼ cup chicken broth

1 pound crawfish tails, peeled

1 tablespoon Creole seasoning

½ teaspoon salt

½ teaspoon ground black pepper

⅛ teaspoon hot sauce

1 tablespoon cooking sherry

4 cups cooked long-grain white rice

¼ cup sliced green onions

¼ cup chopped fresh parsley

1 Press the Sauté button on the Instant Pot®. Add butter to pot and heat 30 seconds. Slowly whisk in flour and cook 5 minutes until browned. Add onion, celery, green pepper, and garlic to pot and heat while stirring for an additional 2 minutes.

2 Add diced tomatoes with juice and stir, scraping any bits on the bottom and sides of pot. Add broth, crawfish, Creole seasoning, salt, pepper, hot sauce, and cooking sherry. Lock lid.

3 Press the Manual or Pressure Cook button and adjust cook time to 8 minutes. When timer beeps, quick-release pressure until float valve drops and then unlock lid.

4 Ladle étouffée into four bowls. Garnish each bowl with 1 cup rice, green onions, and parsley. Serve warm.

Shrimp, Smoked Sausage, and Peppers

This dish will transport you to the bayou. Filling, low in calories, and full of flavor, this recipe will become a favorite in your weekly meal rotation. In addition, this is a great dish to portion out for quick meals or to take to work.

- **Hands-On Time: 5 minutes**
- **Cook Time: 5 minutes**

Serves 4

1 tablespoon olive oil

1 small yellow onion, peeled and diced

½ green bell pepper, seeded and thinly sliced

½ red bell pepper, seeded and thinly sliced

½ yellow bell pepper, seeded and thinly sliced

1 (14.5-ounce) can diced tomatoes, including juice

2 pounds large uncooked shrimp, peeled and deveined

12 ounces smoked sausage, sliced into ½" sections

2 teaspoons Old Bay Seasoning

½ teaspoon salt

½ teaspoon ground black pepper

1 cup water

1 Press the Sauté button on the Instant Pot®. Add oil to pot and heat 30 seconds. Add onion and peppers and sauté 5 minutes until onions are translucent. Add tomatoes with juice, shrimp, sausage, Old Bay Seasoning, salt, pepper, and water. Lock lid.

2 Press the Steam button and adjust time to 0 minutes. When timer beeps, quick-release pressure until float valve drops and then unlock lid.

3 Using a slotted spoon, transfer mixture to four bowls and serve warm.

Old Bay Lobster Tails

Full of essential vitamins, lobster is a great source of protein—tasty and festive protein at that—and is low in calories and saturated fat. Now every week can be a party, and your meal will be complete in minutes!

- **Hands-On Time: 2 minutes**
- **Cook Time: 4 minutes**

Serves 4

1 cup water
1 tablespoon Old Bay Seasoning
4 (6-ounce) uncooked
   lobster tails, thawed
¼ cup unsalted butter, melted

1 Add water and Old Bay Seasoning to the Instant Pot® and insert steamer basket. Add lobster tails to basket. Lock lid.

2 Press the Steam button and adjust time to 4 minutes. When timer beeps, quick-release pressure until float valve drops and then unlock lid.

3 Transfer tails to an ice bath to stop the lobster from overcooking, then remove meat from shells. Serve with melted butter.

Sea Scallops with Cherry Sauce

Make sure you choose sea scallops for this recipe, as bay scallops are small and won't work with the recipe as written. You only need a quick sear on each side of the scallop before steaming so it doesn't overcook and become rubbery.

- **Hands-On Time: 5 minutes**
- **Cook Time: 1 minute**

Serves 2

¼ cup cherry preserves
1 teaspoon lemon juice
1 teaspoon tamari
1 tablespoon unsalted butter
1 pound fresh sea scallops
½ teaspoon salt
1 cup water

1 In a small bowl, whisk together preserves, lemon juice, and tamari. Set aside.

2 Press the Sauté button on the Instant Pot®. Add butter to pot and heat 30 seconds. Season scallops with salt, add to pot, and sear 30 seconds per side. Transfer to steamer basket. Top scallops with preserve mixture.

3 Add water to the Instant Pot®. Insert steamer basket. Lock lid.

4 Press the Manual or Pressure Cook button and adjust cook time to 0 minutes. When timer beeps, quick-release pressure until float valve drops and then unlock lid.

5 Transfer scallops to two plates. Serve warm.

Desserts and Drinks

Just because you can't indulge in gluten doesn't mean that the flavor and joy of desserts and sweet drink treats have to be sacrificed. With so many flour choices and sweet creations, that craving can still be satisfied. Also, the Instant Pot® creates desserts that are just the right size to make your sweet tooth *and* your scale happy. Most of these desserts provide only 4–6 servings, so you won't be tempted to overeat, and you won't have desserts hanging around your kitchen for days on end. With dishes ranging from Espresso Rice Pudding and Raspberry White Chocolate Cocoa to Toffee Chip Brownies and Chocolate Mint Hot Cocoa, these perfect little delights are guaranteed to hit the spot...no matter what you find yourself craving.

Spiced Pear-Applesauce

This is excellent served with pork chops, as an oil replacement in bakery treats, topped on oatmeal, and even as an ingredient in a fancy vinaigrette.

- **Hands-On Time: 20 minutes**
- **Cook Time: 8 minutes**

Yields 10 cups

2 pounds variety of apples, peeled, cored, and chopped

1 tablespoon ground cinnamon

2 whole star anise

6 whole allspice

½ cup freshly squeezed orange juice

⅓ cup light brown sugar

½ teaspoon salt

⅓ cup water

1 Add apples, cinnamon, star anise, whole allspice, orange juice, sugar, salt, and water to the Instant Pot®. Lock lid.

2 Press the Manual or Pressure Cook button and adjust cook time to 8 minutes. When timer beeps, quick-release pressure until float valve drops and then unlock lid.

3 Remove star anise and allspice. Use an immersion blender to blend the ingredients in pot, or use a stand blender to blend applesauce in batches until desired consistency is reached. Serve warm or cold.

Raspberry White Chocolate Cocoa

While the kiddos are throwing snowballs at each other, the adults can find a little escape and warmth with this kicked-up cocoa!

- **Hands-On Time: 5 minutes**
- **Cook Time: 8 minutes**

Serves 4

5 cups whole milk

½ cup white chocolate chips

½ cup Chambord (raspberry liqueur)

⅛ teaspoon salt

2 teaspoons vanilla extract

2 tablespoons granulated sugar

1 Add all ingredients to the Instant Pot®. Lock lid.

2 Press the Steam button and adjust time to 8 minutes. When timer beeps, quick-release pressure until float valve drops and then unlock lid. Whisk ingredients to ensure smoothness.

3 Ladle cocoa into four mugs and serve warm.

Blueberry Compote

Good right off the spoon, over oatmeal or gluten-free pancakes, atop a cheesecake, or with ice cream, this blueberry compote has many uses. Although you can store it for up to a week in the refrigerator, it is doubtful that this scrumptious treat will last that long.

- **Hands-On Time: 10 minutes**
- **Cook Time: 4 minutes**

Serves 4

1 pound fresh blueberries
1 tablespoon granulated sugar
2 tablespoons honey
2 tablespoons orange zest
Juice from 1 medium orange
1 teaspoon vanilla extract
⅛ teaspoon salt
2 tablespoons water
1 teaspoon cornstarch

1 Add blueberries, sugar, honey, orange zest, orange juice, vanilla, salt, and water to the Instant Pot®. Lock lid.

2 Press the Manual or Pressure Cook button and adjust cook time to 4 minutes. When timer beeps, let pressure release naturally for 5 minutes. Quick-release any additional pressure until float valve drops and then unlock lid.

3 Stir in cornstarch to thicken mixture, smooshing blueberries against the sides of the pot as you stir.

4 Transfer blueberry mixture to an airtight container and refrigerate until ready to eat. Serve warm or cold.

Orange-Glazed Blueberry Upside-Down Cake

This supermoist one-layer cake is perfect when you have a sweet tooth but only want a small portion. There is none of the gluten and none of the guilt. The orange glaze makes this recipe a light bite to enjoy with a cup of tea or coffee with friends.

- **Hands-On Time: 15 minutes**
- **Cook Time: 25 minutes**

Serves 6

Cake
1 cup fresh blueberries
1 cup all-purpose gluten-free flour
2 teaspoons gluten-free baking powder
½ teaspoon baking soda
¼ cup granulated sugar
⅛ teaspoon salt
½ teaspoon vanilla extract
3 tablespoons unsalted butter, melted
2 large eggs
2 tablespoons whole milk
1 tablespoon orange zest
2 cups water

Orange Glaze
5 tablespoons granulated sugar
5 teaspoons fresh orange juice, strained of pulp

1 Lightly grease a 7" springform pan with either oil or cooking spray. Pour blueberries into cake pan until the bottom of the pan is covered. Set aside.

2 In a large bowl, combine flour, baking powder, baking soda, sugar, and salt.

3 In a medium bowl, combine vanilla, butter, eggs, milk, and orange zest.

4 Pour wet ingredients from the medium bowl into the large bowl with dry ingredients. Gently combine ingredients. Do not overmix. Spoon mixture into greased cake pan.

5 Add water to the Instant Pot® and insert steam rack. Place pan on top. Lock lid.

6 Press the Manual or Pressure Cook button and adjust cook time to 25 minutes. When timer beeps, quick-release pressure until float valve drops and then unlock lid.

7 Remove pan from pot and set aside to cool 5 minutes. Remove springform side and flip cake onto a serving plate and allow to completely cool 30 minutes.

8 Whisk together glaze ingredients until the consistency of corn syrup. If glaze is too thick, add more juice; if glaze is too runny, add more sugar. Gently pour glaze evenly over cooled cake. Slice cake and serve.

Chocolate Cake with Peanut Butter Ganache

There has never been a marriage as sweet and faithful as the divine duo of peanut butter and chocolate. Using peanut butter chips to make a ganache lends a lighter, silkier touch than using a heavier buttercream. This mini cake is extremely addictive and irresistibly dreamy...and there is no gluten to be found!

- **Hands-On Time: 10 minutes**
- **Cook Time: 20 minutes**

Serves 6

2 large eggs, whisked
1 teaspoon vanilla extract
⅓ cup gluten-free all-purpose flour
2 tablespoons unsweetened cocoa powder
⅓ cup granulated sugar
2 teaspoons gluten-free baking powder
1 teaspoon baking soda
⅛ teaspoon salt
4 tablespoons unsalted butter, melted
2 tablespoons whole milk
⅓ cup semisweet chocolate chips
1 cup water
¼ cup heavy cream
½ cup peanut butter chips

1 In a large bowl, combine eggs, vanilla, flour, cocoa powder, sugar, baking powder, baking soda, and salt. Stir in melted butter and milk and then fold in chocolate chips. Do not overmix. Pour batter into a 6" cake pan greased with either oil or cooking spray.

2 Add water to the Instant Pot®. Insert steam rack. Place cake pan on top of the steam rack. Lock lid.

3 Press the Pressure Cook or Manual button and adjust cook time to 20 minutes. When timer beeps, let pressure release naturally. Quick-release any additional pressure until float valve drops and then unlock lid.

4 Remove cake pan from pot and transfer to a rack to cool 10 minutes. Flip cake onto a serving platter. Let cool completely 30 minutes.

5 In a small saucepan, bring heavy cream to a light rolling boil over medium heat (do not overheat, as it will scorch). Remove from heat. Add peanut butter chips to heated cream and stir until melted. Gently pour ganache over cake. Let set for 30 minutes. Serve.

Strawberry Cupcakes with Vanilla Buttercream

When you don't want to make an entire batch of cupcakes, the Instant Pot® comes to your rescue with simple ingredients and smaller portions. The fresh strawberries are amazing against the rich vanilla buttercream. If you happen to have a vanilla bean, split it open and scrape the pod (approximately ¾ teaspoon) for a tasty alternative.

- **Hands-On Time: 10 minutes**
- **Cook Time: 9 minutes**

Serves 6

Strawberry Cupcakes

1¼ cups gluten-free all-purpose baking flour

2 teaspoons gluten-free baking powder

½ teaspoon baking soda

⅛ teaspoon salt

½ teaspoon vanilla extract

1 teaspoon lime zest

3 tablespoons unsalted butter, melted

2 large eggs

¼ cup granulated sugar

⅓ cup finely diced fresh strawberries, hulled

1 cup water

Vanilla Buttercream

1 cup powdered sugar

⅓ cup unsalted butter, softened

½ teaspoon vanilla extract

2 teaspoons whole milk

1 In a large bowl, combine flour, baking powder, baking soda, and salt.

2 In a medium bowl, combine vanilla, lime zest, butter, eggs, and sugar.

3 Pour wet ingredients from the medium bowl into the large bowl with dry ingredients. Gently combine ingredients. Do not overmix. Fold in strawberries, then spoon mixture into six silicone cupcake liners lightly greased with either oil or cooking spray.

4 Add water to the Instant Pot® and insert steam rack. Place cupcake liners on top. Lock lid.

5 Press the Manual or Pressure Cook button and adjust cook time to 9 minutes. When timer beeps, quick-release pressure until float valve drops and then unlock lid.

6 Remove cupcakes from pot and set aside to cool 20 minutes.

7 Once cupcakes have cooled, cream together powdered sugar, softened butter, vanilla extract, and milk. Spread topping on cooled cupcakes and serve.

Strawberry Buckwheat Cake with Chocolate Ganache

The freshness of the strawberries plays nicely with the rustic personality of the buckwheat in this tasty cake. The silky-smooth chocolate ganache brings it all together with just the right amount of sweetness. This cake is a nice little gluten-free treat after a meal or shared with friends during a morning tea and get-together.

- **Hands-On Time: 15 minutes**
- **Cook Time: 28 minutes**

Serves 6

Cake

1 cup buckwheat flour

2 teaspoons gluten-free baking powder

½ teaspoon baking soda

¼ cup granulated sugar

⅛ teaspoon salt

½ teaspoon vanilla extract

3 tablespoons unsalted butter, melted

2 large eggs

2 tablespoons whole milk

½ cup diced fresh strawberries, hulled

2 cups water

Chocolate Ganache

½ cup heavy cream

9 tablespoons semisweet chocolate chips

⅛ teaspoon salt

1 Lightly grease a 7" springform pan with either oil or cooking spray.

2 In a large bowl, combine flour, baking powder, baking soda, sugar, and salt.

3 In a medium bowl, combine vanilla, butter, eggs, and milk.

4 Pour wet ingredients from the medium bowl into the large bowl with dry ingredients. Gently combine ingredients. Do not overmix. Fold in strawberries. Spoon mixture into greased pan.

5 Add water to the Instant Pot® and insert steam rack. Place cake pan on top. Lock lid.

6 Press the Manual or Pressure Cook button and adjust cook time to 25 minutes. When timer beeps, quick-release pressure until float valve drops and then unlock lid.

7 Remove pan from pot and set aside to cool 5 minutes. Remove springform side and flip cake onto a serving plate and let cool 15 minutes.

8 In a small saucepan, bring heavy cream to a rolling boil over medium heat. Remove from heat. Add chocolate chips and salt. Let stand for 3 minutes. Whisk until smooth. Gently pour ganache over cake. Let set for 30 minutes. Serve.

Red Velvet Cake with Cream Cheese Frosting

The buttermilk and cocoa work together to create a unique chocolate flavor, and the food coloring gives the cake that reddish color. This gluten-free moist mini red velvet cake hits the spot when you are craving this vintage confection topped with the to-die-for cream cheese frosting.

- **Hands-On Time: 10 minutes**
- **Cook Time: 25 minutes**

Serves 6

Cake

1 cup gluten-free all-purpose flour

2 teaspoons gluten-free baking powder

½ teaspoon baking soda

⅓ cup granulated sugar

2 teaspoons unsweetened cocoa powder

⅛ teaspoon salt

2 large eggs, whisked

3 tablespoons unsalted butter, melted and cooled

½ teaspoon vanilla extract

2 tablespoons buttermilk

½ teaspoon apple cider vinegar

8 drops red food coloring

2 cups water

Frosting

4 tablespoons cream cheese, room temperature

4 tablespoons unsalted butter, room temperature

1½ cups powdered sugar

⅛ teaspoon salt

¼ teaspoon vanilla extract

1 Lightly grease a 7" springform pan with either oil or cooking spray.

2 In a large bowl, combine flour, baking powder, baking soda, sugar, cocoa, and salt.

3 In a medium bowl, combine eggs, butter, vanilla, buttermilk, apple cider vinegar, and red food coloring.

4 Pour wet ingredients from the medium bowl into the large bowl with dry ingredients. Gently combine ingredients. Do not overmix. Spoon mixture into greased pan.

5 Add water to the Instant Pot® and insert steam rack. Place cake pan on top. Lock lid.

6 Press the Manual or Pressure Cook button and adjust cook time to 25 minutes. When timer beeps, quick-release pressure until float valve drops and then unlock lid.

7 Remove pan from pot and set aside to cool 5 minutes. Remove springform side and flip cake onto a serving plate and let cool 15 minutes.

8 Cream together frosting ingredients until smooth. Spread frosting over cooled cake. Slice and serve.

Lime Cheesecake

Close your eyes and take a bite. Now open them. Are you in Margaritaville yet? The fresh lime juice and zest will have your taste buds dancing to the best of Jimmy Buffett! Add a drop of green food coloring to lend a little splash of extra flair to this already beautiful summer dessert.

- **Hands-On Time: 10 minutes**
- **Cook Time: 30 minutes**

Serves 6

Crust
1 cup crushed Rice Chex
1 tablespoon granulated sugar
1 teaspoon lime zest
3 tablespoons unsalted butter, melted
⅛ teaspoon salt

Cheesecake Filling
12 ounces cream cheese, cubed and room temperature
2 tablespoons sour cream, room temperature
½ cup granulated sugar
2 large eggs, room temperature
Zest of 2 large limes
1 tablespoon fresh lime juice
1 teaspoon vanilla extract
2 cups water

1. **For Crust:** Grease a 7" springform pan with either oil or cooking spray and set aside.

2. In a small bowl, combine Rice Chex, sugar, lime zest, butter, and salt. Transfer crumb mixture to springform pan and press down along the bottom and one-third of the way up the sides of the pan. Place a square of aluminum foil along the outside of the bottom of the pan and crimp up around the edges.

3. **For Cheesecake Filling:** Using a hand blender or food processor, cream together cream cheese, sour cream, and sugar. Pulse until smooth. Slowly add eggs, lime zest, lime juice, and vanilla. Pulse another 10 seconds. Scrape the bowl and pulse until batter is smooth.

4. Transfer batter to springform pan.

5. Add water to the Instant Pot®. Insert steam rack. Set the springform pan on the steam rack. Lock lid.

6. Press Manual or Pressure Cook button and adjust cook time to 30 minutes. When timer beeps, quick-release pressure until float valve drops and then unlock lid.

7. Remove cake pan from pot. Let cool at room temperature 10 minutes. Cheesecake will be a little jiggly in the center. Refrigerate at least 2 hours to allow it to set. Release side pan and serve.

Vanilla Bean Cheesecake

Thick and creamy, this cheesecake may be mini, but it is definitely mighty! Although vanilla extract can be used, using a vanilla bean ramps up the flavor three notches. And the gluten-free crust is divine with its touch of citrus from the lemon zest.

- Hands-On Time: 10 minutes
- Cook Time: 30 minutes

Serves 6

Whipped Topping
½ cup heavy whipping cream
Seeds of ½ vanilla bean
2 tablespoons powdered sugar

Crust
1 cup crushed Cheerios
1 tablespoon light brown sugar
1 teaspoon lemon zest
3 tablespoons unsalted butter, melted
⅛ teaspoon salt

Cheesecake Filling
12 ounces cream cheese, cubed and room temperature
2 tablespoons sour cream, room temperature
½ cup granulated sugar
2 large eggs, room temperature
Seeds of 1½ vanilla beans
2 cups water

1 **For Whipped Topping:** In a large metal bowl, whip cream until soft peaks form. Add vanilla bean seeds and whip 30 seconds. Add sugar and whip until stiff peaks form. Refrigerate covered until ready to serve.

2 **For Crust:** Grease a 7" springform pan with either oil or cooking spray and set aside.

3 In a small bowl, combine crushed Cheerios, brown sugar, lemon zest, butter, and salt. Transfer crumb mixture to springform pan and press down along the bottom and one-third of the way up the sides of the pan. Place a square of aluminum foil along the outside of the bottom of the pan and crimp up around the edges.

4 **For Cheesecake Filling:** Using a hand blender or food processor, cream together cream cheese, sour cream, and sugar. Pulse until smooth. Slowly add eggs and vanilla beans. Scrape the bowl and pulse until batter is smooth. Transfer batter to springform pan.

5 Add water to the Instant Pot®. Insert steam rack. Set the springform pan on the steam rack. Lock lid.

6 Press the Manual or Pressure Cook button and adjust cook time to 30 minutes. When timer beeps, quick-release pressure until float valve drops and then unlock lid.

7 Remove pan from pot. Let cool at room temperature 10 minutes. Cheesecake will be a little jiggly in the center. Refrigerate at least 2 hours to allow it to set. Release side pan and serve with whipped topping.

Raspberry Cake with Lemon Glaze

Bursting with flavor from raspberries and lemon, this little cake just screams summer. The light, citrusy glaze complements the berry cake in delicious perfection. Small in size, this dessert is ideal when you want a little something sweet, but don't want the leftovers of a bigger, traditional cake lingering in your home all week. Enjoy a slice with a morning cup of coffee or tea.

- **Hands-On Time: 10 minutes**
- **Cook Time: 30 minutes**

Serves 6

Cake
2 large eggs
3 tablespoons whole milk
2 tablespoons lemon juice
1 teaspoon lemon zest
4 tablespoons unsalted butter, melted and cooled
1⅓ cups gluten-free all-purpose flour
1½ teaspoons gluten-free baking powder
½ teaspoon baking soda
½ cup granulated sugar
⅛ teaspoon salt
½ cup halved fresh raspberries
1 cup water

Lemon Glaze
5 tablespoons powdered sugar
5 teaspoons fresh lemon juice

1. Lightly grease a 7" springform pan with either oil or cooking spray.

2. In a medium bowl, whisk together eggs, milk, lemon juice, lemon zest, and butter.

3. In a large bowl, combine flour, baking powder, baking soda, sugar, salt, and raspberries.

4. Pour wet ingredients from the medium bowl into the large bowl with dry ingredients. Using a fork, cream together mixture until combined. Do not overmix, as some lumps are fine.

5. Transfer mixture to greased springform pan.

6. Add water to the Instant Pot® and insert steam rack. Place springform pan on top. Lock lid.

7. Press the Manual or Pressure Cook button and adjust cook time to 30 minutes. When timer beeps, quick-release pressure until float valve drops and then unlock lid.

8. Unlock springform pan and let cool completely 30 minutes.

9. Whisk together glaze ingredients until the consistency of corn syrup. If glaze is too thick, add more juice; if glaze is too runny, add more sugar. Gently pour glaze evenly over cooled cake. Slice and serve.

Spiced Pumpkin Custard

With pumpkin mania all around and in every product on the shelves, you can make this gluten-free delight to satisfy your craving. To take this special pumpkin treat over the top, serve with fresh whipped cream and crushed gluten-free cinnamon cereal or graham crackers for the crust. Most graham crackers on the market today are unfortunately made with wheat flour; however, there are hundreds of delicious gluten-free graham cracker recipes on the Internet to play with!

- **Hands-On Time: 15 minutes**
- **Cook Time: 19 minutes**

Serves 4

4 large egg yolks

2 tablespoons granulated sugar

1 teaspoon pumpkin pie spice

⅛ teaspoon salt

¼ teaspoon vanilla extract

1½ cups heavy cream

¾ cup canned pumpkin

2 cups water

1 In a small bowl, whisk together egg yolks, sugar, pumpkin pie spice, salt, and vanilla. Set aside.

2 In a saucepan over medium-low heat, heat cream 3 minutes to a low simmer. Whisk 1 teaspoon cream into egg mixture to temper it, then slowly whisk egg mixture into the saucepan with remaining cream. Add pumpkin and continually stir at a simmer 10 minutes until combined. Remove pan from heat and evenly distribute pumpkin mixture among four custard ramekins.

3 Add water to the Instant Pot®. Insert steam rack. Place silicone steamer basket onto steam rack. Place ramekins in steamer basket. Lock lid.

4 Press Manual button and adjust cook time to 6 minutes. When timer beeps, let pressure release naturally for 10 minutes. Quick-release any additional pressure until float valve drops and then unlock lid.

5 Transfer custards to a plate and refrigerate covered 2 hours until set. Serve.

Dark Chocolate Crème Brûlée

We all know that you need a blowtorch for a great crème brûlée. But what if you actually don't? Place your custard ramekins in an ice bath (water and ice) in an oven-safe dish. Broil at 500°F for 2 minutes until tops are browned. The ice bath keeps the custard from cooking while the broiler works its magic on the top sugar layer!

- **Hands-On Time: 15 minutes**
- **Cook Time: 19 minutes**

Serves 4

4 large egg yolks
2 tablespoons granulated sugar
⅛ teaspoon salt
¼ teaspoon vanilla extract
1½ cups heavy cream
¾ cup dark chocolate chips
2 cups water
½ cup superfine sugar

SUPERFINE SUGAR

Superfine sugar has smaller granules than typical granulated sugar and is sold in most stores. If you don't have time to run to the store, just pulse your granulated sugar in a small food processor to achieve the same result.

1 In a small bowl, whisk together egg yolks, sugar, salt, and vanilla. Set aside.

2 In a saucepan over medium-low heat, bring cream to a low simmer 3 minutes. Whisk 1 teaspoon cream into the egg mixture to temper it, then slowly add egg mixture into the saucepan with remaining cream. Add dark chocolate chips and continually stir at a simmer 10 minutes until chocolate is melted. Remove from heat and evenly distribute mixture among four custard ramekins.

3 Add water to the Instant Pot®. Insert steam rack. Place silicone steamer basket onto steam rack. Place ramekins in steamer basket. Lock lid.

4 Press Manual button and adjust cook time to 6 minutes. When timer beeps, let pressure release naturally for 10 minutes. Quick-release any additional pressure until float valve drops and then unlock lid.

5 Transfer custards to a plate and refrigerate covered 2 hours.

6 Right before serving, top custards with equal amounts superfine sugar. Use a blowtorch on the tops (or broil custards) to create a caramelized shell. Serve.

Toffee Chip Brownies

The word *decadent* doesn't do these little gems justice. Brownies on their own are the perfect dessert, but by adding the buttery, crunchy toffee chips, this chocolate confection is taken to an entire new dimension. And kudos to you if the batter actually makes it to your pan, as "by the spoonful" is another tempting way to enjoy these brownies!

- **Hands-On Time: 10 minutes**
- **Cook Time: 20 minutes**

Serves 6

2 large eggs, whisked
1 teaspoon vanilla extract
¼ cup gluten-free all-purpose flour
¼ cup unsweetened cocoa powder
⅓ cup granulated sugar
2 teaspoons gluten-free baking powder
1 teaspoon baking soda
⅛ teaspoon salt
4 tablespoons unsalted butter, room temperature
2 tablespoons whole milk
⅓ cup English toffee bits
1 cup water

1 In a large bowl, combine eggs, vanilla, flour, cocoa powder, sugar, baking powder, baking soda, and salt. Stir in melted butter and milk and then fold in toffee bits. Do not overmix. Pour batter into a 6" cake pan greased with either oil or cooking spray.

2 Add water to the Instant Pot®. Insert steam rack. Place cake pan on top of the steam rack. Lock lid.

3 Press the Pressure Cook or Manual button and adjust cook time to 20 minutes. When timer beeps, let pressure release naturally. Quick-release any additional pressure until float valve drops and then unlock lid.

4 Remove cake pan from pot and transfer to a rack to cool 10 minutes. Flip cake onto a serving platter. Let cool completely 30 minutes. Slice and serve.

Espresso Rice Pudding

You know that Arborio rice is heavenly in risotto due to its extra-starchy quality, but you won't believe the creaminess that this rice lends to pudding. The addition of rich and luxurious espresso powder is perfect for coffee lovers.

- **Hands-On Time: 10 minutes**
- **Cook Time: 15 minutes**

Serves 8

1 cup Arborio rice

1½ cups water

1 teaspoon instant espresso powder

1 teaspoon vanilla extract

1 tablespoon unsalted butter

⅓ cup raisins

⅛ teaspoon ground cinnamon

⅛ teaspoon salt

⅓ cup light brown sugar

½ cup whole milk

2 large eggs

1. Add rice, water, espresso powder, vanilla, and butter to the Instant Pot®. Lock lid.

2. Press the Manual or Pressure Cook button and adjust cook time to 10 minutes. When timer beeps, let pressure release naturally for 5 minutes. Quick-release any additional pressure until float valve drops and then unlock lid.

3. Stir in raisins, cinnamon, salt, and brown sugar.

4. In a medium bowl, whisk together milk and eggs. Add 1 tablespoon of rice mixture to eggs, stirring quickly to temper. Quickly stir mixture in medium bowl back into pot, ensuring eggs don't scramble.

5. Let mixture simmer unlidded 5 minutes. Transfer to eight bowls and serve warm.

ARE MY EGGS FRESH?

If you're not sure if the eggs in your refrigerator are fresh enough to consume, try this little kitchen hack: fill a bowl with water and add your egg. If it sinks to the bottom, it is fresh. If it floats to the top, it is past the consumption date. Boom—it's that easy.

Spiced Chai Latte

Your friends will think they just stopped by their favorite local teahouse when they taste the freshness and richness of this homemade chai. The fragrant spices will fill your home with warmth, and the chai latte will fill your tummy with creamy goodness.

- **Hands-On Time: 5 minutes**
- **Cook Time: 15 minutes**

Serves 4

3 cups water
4 black tea bags
3 cardamom pods
4 whole cloves
1 cinnamon stick
4 whole allspice
¼ teaspoon ground nutmeg
¼ teaspoon ground ginger
1 cup whole milk
¼ cup granulated sugar

1 Add water, tea bags, cardamom, cloves, cinnamon stick, allspice, nutmeg, and ginger to the Instant Pot®. Lock lid.

2 Press the Steam button and adjust time to 10 minutes. When timer beeps, quick-release pressure until float valve drops and then unlock lid.

3 Add milk and sugar to pot and let steep an additional 5 minutes. Strain. Press any additional liquid and flavor out of the tea bags. Serve warm, chilled, or on ice.

Chocolate Mint Hot Cocoa

Don't forget the mini marshmallows for this recipe! But beware and read the labels, as some marshmallows contain a starch that has gluten. Of course, there is always fresh whipped cream!

- **Hands-On Time: 5 minutes**
- **Cook Time: 8 minutes**

Serves 4

6 cups whole milk
¼ cup unsweetened cocoa powder
¼ cup chocolate mint chips
¼ cup granulated sugar
⅛ teaspoon salt
2 teaspoons vanilla extract

1 Add all ingredients to the Instant Pot®. Lock lid.

2 Press the Steam button and adjust time to 8 minutes. When timer beeps, quick-release pressure until float valve drops and then unlock lid. Whisk ingredients to ensure smoothness.

3 Ladle cocoa into four mugs and serve warm.

Mini Mochaccino Cheesecakes

When you need your cheesecake, chocolate, and coffee all in one, and you need it to go, grab one of these mini desserts and hit the road. Your taste buds will never know that with every indulgent bite these cheesecakes are gluten-free, down to the chocolatey crust!

- **Hands-On Time: 5 minutes**
- **Cook Time: 20 minutes**

Serves 6

Crust

½ cup old-fashioned oats

8 whole raw almonds

¼ cup unsweetened cocoa

2 tablespoons granulated sugar

3 tablespoons unsalted butter, melted

⅛ teaspoon salt

Cheesecake Filling

6 ounces cream cheese, cubed and room temperature

1 tablespoon sour cream, room temperature

¼ teaspoon vanilla extract

2 teaspoons instant espresso powder

¼ cup granulated sugar

1 large egg, room temperature

1 cup water

1 **For Crust:** Lightly grease six silicone cupcake liners with either oil or cooking spray.

2 In a small food processor, pulse oats, almonds, unsweetened cocoa, sugar, butter, and salt. Transfer crumb mixture to liners and press down along the bottom and one-third of the way up the sides of the pan.

3 **For Cheesecake Filling:** Using a hand blender or food processor, cream together cream cheese, sour cream, vanilla, espresso powder, and sugar. Pulse until smooth. Slowly add egg. Pulse 10 seconds. Scrape the bowl and pulse until batter is smooth. Transfer batter into silicone cupcake liners.

4 Add water to the Instant Pot®. Insert steam rack. Place steamer basket on steam rack. Carefully place cheesecakes in steamer basket. Lock lid.

5 Press the Manual or Pressure Cook button and adjust cook time to 20 minutes. When timer beeps, quick-release pressure until float valve drops and then unlock lid.

6 Remove steamer basket from pot. Let cheesecakes cool at room temperature 10 minutes.

7 Cheesecakes will be a little jiggly in the center. Refrigerate at least 1 hour to allow them to set.

Blackberry Crisp

This delicious Blackberry Crisp is the perfect pick-me-up for those rainy summer days. Scoop this right out of the Instant Pot® and into your bowl and top with vanilla or cinnamon ice cream or some freshly made whipped cream. This is sure to cure any blues that may be ailing you!

- **Hands-On Time: 15 minutes**
- **Cook Time: 8 minutes**

Serves 4

Blackberry Filling

2 cups fresh blackberries
¼ cup water
1 tablespoon freshly
    squeezed orange juice
¼ cup granulated sugar
1 teaspoon cornstarch
1 teaspoon cinnamon
¼ teaspoon ground nutmeg
⅛ teaspoon salt

Topping

4 tablespoons unsalted
    butter, melted
1 cup old-fashioned oats
⅛ cup gluten-free all-
    purpose flour
¼ cup chopped almonds
¼ cup packed light brown
    sugar
¼ teaspoon salt

1 **For Blackberry Filling:** Add filling ingredients to the Instant Pot®. Stir to evenly distribute ingredients.

2 **For Topping:** Mix topping ingredients together in a small bowl. Spoon drops of topping over filling in pot. Lock lid.

3 Press the Manual button and adjust cook time to 8 minutes. When timer beeps, let pressure release naturally until float valve drops and then unlock lid.

4 Spoon crisp into four bowls and enjoy.

US/Metric Conversion Chart

VOLUME CONVERSIONS

US Volume Measure	Metric Equivalent
⅛ teaspoon	0.5 milliliter
¼ teaspoon	1 milliliter
½ teaspoon	2 milliliters
1 teaspoon	5 milliliters
½ tablespoon	7 milliliters
1 tablespoon (3 teaspoons)	15 milliliters
2 tablespoons (1 fluid ounce)	30 milliliters
¼ cup (4 tablespoons)	60 milliliters
⅓ cup	90 milliliters
½ cup (4 fluid ounces)	125 milliliters
⅔ cup	160 milliliters
¾ cup (6 fluid ounces)	180 milliliters
1 cup (16 tablespoons)	250 milliliters
1 pint (2 cups)	500 milliliters
1 quart (4 cups)	1 liter (about)

WEIGHT CONVERSIONS

US Weight Measure	Metric Equivalent
½ ounce	15 grams
1 ounce	30 grams
2 ounces	60 grams
3 ounces	85 grams
¼ pound (4 ounces)	115 grams
½ pound (8 ounces)	225 grams
¾ pound (12 ounces)	340 grams
1 pound (16 ounces)	454 grams

OVEN TEMPERATURE CONVERSIONS

Degrees Fahrenheit	Degrees Celsius
200 degrees F	95 degrees C
250 degrees F	120 degrees C
275 degrees F	135 degrees C
300 degrees F	150 degrees C
325 degrees F	160 degrees C
350 degrees F	180 degrees C
375 degrees F	190 degrees C
400 degrees F	205 degrees C
425 degrees F	220 degrees C
450 degrees F	230 degrees C

BAKING PAN SIZES

American	Metric
8 x 1½ inch round baking pan	20 x 4 cm cake tin
9 x 1½ inch round baking pan	23 x 3.5 cm cake tin
11 x 7 x 1½ inch baking pan	28 x 18 x 4 cm baking tin
13 x 9 x 2 inch baking pan	30 x 20 x 5 cm baking tin
2 quart rectangular baking dish	30 x 20 x 3 cm baking tin
15 x 10 x 2 inch baking pan	30 x 25 x 2 cm baking tin (Swiss roll tin)
9 inch pie plate	22 x 4 or 23 x 4 cm pie plate
7 or 8 inch springform pan	18 or 20 cm springform or loose bottom cake tin
9 x 5 x 3 inch loaf pan	23 x 13 x 7 cm or 2 lb narrow loaf or pate tin
1½ quart casserole	1.5 liter casserole
2 quart casserole	2 liter casserole

Index

About the Author

Michelle Fagone is a recipe developer, mother of two, food blogger, and the author of The "I Love My Instant Pot®" Recipe Book and The "I Love My Instant Pot®" Paleo Recipe Book. On her site, CavegirlCuisine.com, Michelle shares recipes and knowledge about the health benefits of cooking with local, fresh, unprocessed foods. Despite being a southern gal at heart, her travel and food experiences as a navy brat and current army spouse have given her a unique appreciation for worldly flavors. While comfort is the basis of most of her recipes, you will often find a twist of exciting flavors and combinations that make her recipes not only appealing to a broad audience but also uniquely delicious! Cavegirl Cuisine was named one of the Top 50 Paleo Blogs of 2012 by the Institute for the Psychology of Eating. Michelle lives in Louisville, Kentucky.

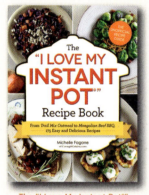
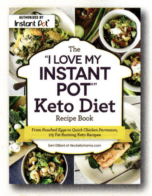
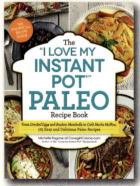
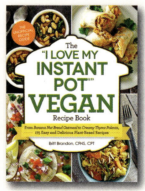
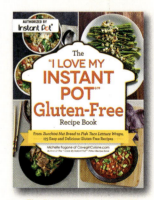